Six Words Of Love

Planes, Scooters, Bikes and Diving
Not Just Surviving, I Choose Thriving

*Enjoy! :)
Lisa O. Brearley*

LISA BREARLEY

First published by Ultimate World Publishing 2023
Copyright © 2023 Lisa Brearley

ISBN

Paperback: 978-1-922982-52-0
Ebook: 978-1-922982-53-7

Lisa Brearley has asserted her rights under the Copyright, Designs and Patents Act 1988 to be identified as the author of this work. The information in this book is based on the author's experiences and opinions. The publisher specifically disclaims responsibility for any adverse consequences which may result from use of the information contained herein. Permission to use information has been sought by the author. Any breaches will be rectified in further editions of the book.

All rights reserved. No part of this publication may be reproduced, stored in or introduced into a retrieval system, or transmitted in any form, or by any means (electronic, mechanical, photocopying, recording or otherwise) without the prior written permission of the author. Any person who does any unauthorized act in relation to this publication may be liable to criminal prosecution and civil claims for damages. Enquiries should be made through the publisher.

Cover design: Ultimate World Publishing
Layout and typesetting: Ultimate World Publishing
Editor: Carmela Julian Valencia

Ultimate World Publishing
Diamond Creek,
Victoria Australia 3089
www.writeabook.com.au

Testimonials

I would like to congratulate my daughter, Lisa, in celebrating her first book (*A Year of Love*) and now her second book (*Six Months of Love*). Lisa is a very capable writer, and I am excited for her to share her life experiences. Lisa is a much-loved teacher to many children. I'm excited for her to write children's books too. I wish Lisa all the best with her writing endeavours and the new adventures that she takes on.

Much love & support,

Peter Gallant, Lisa's dad

Lisa is calm and steady toward what she wants. She has figured out a way to coexist and support a lover in a way that is just beautiful. The dialogue in the book is a beautiful representation of how a supportive relationship can look, not without its hiccups, of course, but with an overarching vision to support the other in becoming their best version.

She is very positive and looks at the good in all situations. She is successfully following her dreams, and that is so inspiring to both me and the readers.

Having met Lisa and Scott at a personal growth course, I know they are committed to growing. We spent ninety days through thick and thin, with constant feedback as to how we were showing up in our lives for ourselves and others. I can see how Lisa and Scott are graceful mirrors for one another to acknowledge some powerful belief systems that exist within everyone.

Lisa brings a humble feminine grace to this book and all aspects of her life.

Carrie-Anne Arand, friend & CEO of Illuminate Leadership Coaching and Training

Over the past year, I have had the privilege of witnessing her determination and relentless work ethic firsthand. Despite the challenges or any obstacles she has faced, Lisa has consistently demonstrated her commitment to her goal and has managed to stay connected to her vision even while travelling the world. What sets Lisa apart is her unparalleled work ethic. She approaches every task with passion, constantly seeking innovative solutions and pushing the boundaries of her abilities. She never shies away from challenges and tackles them head-on, using her creative thinking skills to devise unique strategies for success. Lisa's persistence and determination have been an inspiration to me and everyone fortunate enough to collaborate with her. She possesses an unwavering drive to achieve excellence, constantly going above and beyond to ensure the success of her book launch. Her unwavering dedication to publishing her book, paired with her ability to stay focused on her vision while traversing the globe, has been nothing short of remarkable. I am confident in her ability to excel and make a positive impact wherever she goes and grateful to call her my friend. Keep going Lisa, the best is yet to come!!

Matt Baumann, High Performance Coach, dedicated father, Serial Entrepreneur, CEO and part-time Superhero

Six Months of Love

Bikes, planes, scooters and diving

Not just surviving, I choose thriving

Dedication

Six Months of Love is a book for the one who wants to really tackle life, look at why things happen and make decisions in their life that will give them different results.

I wrote this book for me, to leave a legacy, to inspire, to be heard, to be seen and be proud of it all.

Six Months of Love, an understanding that life is short and the need to really live my life is a priority, is written for me and for you.

Contents

Testimonials	iii
Dedication	vii
Prologue	1
CHAPTER 1: August 2022	13
CHAPTER 2: September 2022	27
CHAPTER 3: October 2022	39
CHAPTER 4: November 2022	53
CHAPTER 5: December 2022	81
CHAPTER 6: January 2023	101
CHAPTER 7: February 2023	119
CHAPTER 8: March 2023	131
CHAPTER 9: April 2023	147
Calls to Action	159
Acknowledgements	161
About the Author	163

Prologue

After this last year of love and a wedding planned in less than three weeks, Scott and I started off on a rough note. If you have read my first book, *A Year of Love*, you have read about all the ups and downs of my personal journey through this thing called life and how it was all interweaved through the most special relationship I have ever experienced with my husband, Scott.

As a writer and storyteller, I've decided that the best way to retell this amazing life journey is through a sequential manner. I've concluded that I have a poor memory and have blamed it on many things. First of all, I thought I was just born with a poor memory. Secondly, I've chalked it up to my past traumas—traumas that have somehow affected what I choose to remember—or an emotional blockage from my past I need to release. I continue to share my concern about my poor memory so that I can discover the inner reason. This challenge of remembering events, places and important information can be very frustrating. So, I present to you in this book the next "chapter" of my life.

Following my first book, *A Year of Love*—where I have weaved through my personal growth journey to finally marrying my soulmate, Scott—this book, *Six Months of Love*, entails our big road trip across North America and our six months in Thailand.

I know you are doing the math right now and saying, "Hey, Lisa, that's more than six months of love." You are totally correct. In this book, you will hear all about our six months in Thailand plus our major biking trip, because you deserve to hear the whole story.

Now, this prologue is the twenty-four hours after our wedding.

Within twenty-four hours of marrying Scott, our marriage seemed to start off on the wrong foot. Well, it was a rough start, and as you may surmise from my growth so far, it's now my perspective to look at challenges and ask the real *why*.

On July 23, 2022, we had a spectacular wedding filled with friends, family and love. I could not ask for anything more. Since our wedding was planned in less than three weeks, we had not planned a getaway (a honeymoon suite with rose petals and a bubble bath) for the evening of our wedding; we stayed put in our Calgary house for our honeymoon.

If you have read my first book, you may recall our dogs. Scott came into my life with his Jack Russell, Norton—a spunky, fun little 15-pound guy. Scott raised him as a pup and loved his Jack Russells—having had two previous, Tymer and Gemma.

Meanwhile, I had an 80-pound Great Pyrenees mix named Alya, whom we rescued from the Calgary Humane Society. She came with her own challenges, and when Scott met then-seven-year-old Alya, she had been with me and my former husband and two kids for just under two years. Alya was a sneak, that's for sure. When a door was

Prologue

opened, she would run. If a gate was left open, she would run. If her harness came off, she would run. It was a learning curve for sure, especially for me as a first-time dog owner.

When we chose Alya, my daughter Brianna was looking for a companion, and we may not have been fully prepared to train and handle an 80-pound dog. And because of how Alya came to the Humane Society (seized by police), we didn't really know her past experiences. However, we fell in love with her from the first time we met her. It was love at first sight.

Okay, back to the twenty-four hours post-wedding. We woke up on the 24th, the day after the wedding, made breakfast for the few friends who stayed at our house in Calgary and decided to ride out with them for an hour or so to see them off on their way back to British Columbia.

After a busy previous day, we were all packed up for a pleasant bike ride. It was a beautiful sunny day, and I looked forward to our first ride together as Mr. and Mrs. Brearley. We were geared up in our leathers and protective gear, and as summer was approaching, it was starting to get a little hot in the dry heat that Calgary, Alberta is known for.

Unfortunately, one of our friends had left the door to the garage open, and the larger door was also open, with the bikes all geared up to go. Seeing this, Alya took the opportunity to escape, almost as if yelling back at us down the alley, "I'll teach you to neglect me on your wedding day, and now you're off on a little bike ride with your friends. I'm outta here!"

We didn't neglect her on our wedding day; however, she and Norton spent time in the cool downstairs, where they would not escape and eat the munchies on the table set out for all our guests to eat.

In the past, when Alya made her escape, I could typically "trick" her into coming back by shaking a bag of dog treats. However, this was not working this time. She was bound and determined for some much-needed attention since she felt neglected. She shot off like a bullet down the alley, behind garages, beside houses, under bushes, and darted faster when I got nearer.

I remained calm, surmising that it was the only way to send some sort of message to Alya that I was the one in control, even though she was obviously the one in the driver's seat. However, this sort of behaviour from a dog is a huge no-no for Scott. As I told him how I managed to get Alya back in the past, he instantly replied, "That's not right. You don't give treats to a dog when they've run away."

Well, the intelligent part of my brain knew that he was 100 percent right. However, at that moment, we just wanted to go for a bike ride and get this dog back as quickly as possible. Our biker friends were ready to go, sweatin' their butts off with their full gear on, and I was out doing my best to rally the troops (okay, just get Alya back to the house).

When Scott realized I was running around aimlessly, doing my best to track down this 80-pound dog, his Spidey sense of knowing this misbehaving dog was being a jerk combined with "I'm not bowing down to this dog to give him treats when I catch him" was brewing inside. And I could feel it from Scott and see it all happening in front of me.

In the past, I've had my own experiences of almost literally wrestling Alya to get her and put a leash on her so she would not run off when I got close. At least twenty minutes of running around the neighbourhood and Alya teasing us with her mischievous personality were getting on Scott's last nerve, and his level of frustration was

Prologue

becoming apparent. So, when he came close to her, he got her by the scruff of her neck, and Alya bit his hand, causing him to bleed quite a bit. That bite was another tick against her on Scott's list of reasons to let her just run off and wish her well. I was watching a level of frustration in Scott that I had never seen before.

When we finally got hold of Alya, it was quite the scene as we cornered her under a bush. With bated breath, hunched-over backs and extremely upset dispositions, we led Alya back to the house. We were both so disappointed in her, tired from the chase and so frustrated that this was her "wedding gift" to us. Gee, thanks, Alya.

This was not easy. Not easy for Scott, and not easy for me. I had seen a side of Scott that I had not seen before. I knew we needed to talk about it; however, our friends were waiting. So, off on the bike trip we went, and Alya was banished down to the basement.

While sitting on the back of Scott's Harley, I soon felt that our first day as the Brearleys was not starting out well. The ride was not smooth because of the incident with Alya. One rough patch led to another and then another, and it's funny how this happened. One of our buddies who was riding behind us almost didn't stop in time when we had to stop quickly at a red light. That was freaky. Then, he didn't realize he was getting low on gas, and we had to figure out where we would stop to fill up. That was annoying. Then, another buddy pulled off the road to pee and didn't tell us, so we pulled around to find him and encountered a guy doing the same maneuver but hesitated to turn quickly, which set off another frustration with Scott.

I could see Scott's frustration compounding. I wasn't sure where I stood. I knew that he could not hear me or anyone else at that point. It made me question how I was going to step up. What decision could (and would) I make in that circumstance? I had never really been in a situation where I needed to decide how to react and say something.

As we headed back home, another rough patch, which could have been deadly, happened. We almost had a head-on collision with another motorcyclist who decided it was fine to pass into oncoming traffic—and we were the oncoming traffic! Fortunately, with Scott's experience, he held his bike steady and confidently kept our bike exactly in our lane. The biker veered off beside us and off into the ditch. He was fine, and so were we.

While riding back home and sitting behind Scott, I took time to think. How would people typically respond to Scott in the past when he was having a bad day? From what he had told me, he never really had anyone see his side, how he felt or how broken he was. No one gave him space to process and then move forward in life. I was not going to be like *all* the other people in his life whom he felt didn't really see him.

At that moment, getting irate or playing some blame game was not the position I wanted to take with Scott. I was not there to blow up at him, nor was I in this new relationship to not say anything.

While riding on the back, I made a decision. I chose to just be with him. I chose to touch his back, hug him, blow him kisses and take time to breathe and think positive thoughts—like how much I loved this man and how I wanted him to know that I was there as his partner, not someone who would just react. I wanted to support him through his journey of self-discovery and growth. I wanted to show up differently in this relationship.

When we got back, it was time to decompress and let our frustrations and feelings just *be* in that moment. Throughout that

Prologue

day, we did not talk any further about how Alya escaped and the stress it caused.

I believe we have come to an understanding that we are *not*—and I repeat—*not* ever going to let concerns or feelings get swept under the rug. We understand that sometimes we just need time to process. We need time to think. We need breathing time, so we can talk to each other with love and purpose and be open to hearing and understanding each other.

In my last book, I talked extensively about the fact that with Scott and me, communication is key. If we don't communicate, we will not make our relationship work. Well, over this year, I've learned that this is the key. *Communication is the key to a strong relationship.* I've learned that we also need to communicate with each other about discussing important matters, even if we can't do it at the exact moment it happens. And that's okay. We *must* talk about what is bothering us, or else we will accumulate resentments or feelings that will not serve our relationship well.

Over this past year, I've also learned to take risks and—this is a huge one for me—tell how I feel, knowing that I don't have an answer and that there is no blame or finger-pointing. When we talk, it's an opportunity for growth. What can we learn from this? What can we be more aware of? How can we be more supportive of each other?

Scott and I know we both come to this relationship with past experiences and stories we have come to believe about ourselves, and they affect how we interact with each other. We talk openly about that. This has been one of the most rewarding parts of our relationship. I'm learning about myself more and more each day and how I step up to be the best partner and soulmate.

I know you want to hear more about how Scott is my soulmate, and when you purchase my first book, *A Year of Love*, you can see how we were and still are each other's soulmate, partner, lover and united forever.

The next time we thoroughly discussed that day was with our online coach and therapist, Kimberly. We found working with her extremely beneficial on an individual and partner level, as we had many sessions together and individually. Kimberly supported our conversation about this rough day, and I had two concerns that arose from it.

First of all, I know Scott and I are growing as individuals and as a couple. I wanted to know how to support and love him on those challenging days. The days when he had so much doubt about himself and life just happens because, like many of us, we do what we know. Secondly, I struggled with learning how to be heard in those situations without creating any doubt of the love I still feel for him. I have a strong tie to Scott, and I truly have remained open and honest with him that I'm learning every day. And I will continue to love him through his growth, as I've experienced him loving me through my own growth.

Over this year, I have learned that one way I can love him best is to remain in his loving space yet still give him the space he needs; sounds like a complicated idea, however, I feel we do our best with this for each other.

During our session with Kimberly, I shared how I felt that day on the back of Scott's bike. I was struggling with the feeling of helplessness, of being a passenger on the back of his bike while he was not grounded or centred, which ramps up my stress. I trust Scott's ability to ride; he has proven to me that he is a highly capable rider. But at the same time, I've heard about so many bike accidents, and I felt "naked" on the bike—so open to being easily hurt, thrown off, run into and so on.

Prologue

In this safe and calm space with Kimberly, Scott heard me. Over the next few months, we had time to talk so much more about this. When we were on the bike, Scott often took the time to see how I was feeling by checking in with a quick thumbs up and caressing my leg. I, too, would rub his back and blow him kisses. I had time to get to know him more as a rider and let go and trust. All the past stories of accidents on a motorcycle made me hesitant to ride on the back of his bike. I knew that I needed to trust him and just enjoy the ride. I often considered this comparison to acknowledge and gauge how I handled riding on the back of his bike: If I was a passenger in a car, I easily trust the driver, so why shouldn't I trust Scott riding the motorcycle?

Genuinely communicating about our challenges has continued to be a top priority in our relationship, and this never changed over the two-month biking adventure in the summer and our six-month stay in Thailand. So let me tell you about this biking trip across Canada and the United States, which was not fully planned. Yes, you heard me—not fully planned. All I needed to remind myself was that "We got this!" and, you may remember from my last book, to remain open.

In a nutshell, Scott rode east across Canada on his sexy, orange Road Glide Harley Davidson to Prince Edward Island, the smallest province on the east side of Canada, where I grew up. We were meeting up with all my family during the month of August 2022. I flew there to meet him, then we rode back to Calgary across the US and Canada. I'll get into that amazing adventure in the next chapter.

Over the next nine chapters, I will be explicit about the range of emotions that have travelled through me during those months. This is one of the coolest areas of growth that I have experienced since meeting Scott. This may sound odd to you, or maybe you resonate with this, but most of my life I've shown and shared a very limited range of emotions, especially sadness. Since meeting Scott, I've broadened my range of expression, and it feels great. Best of all, he respects and supports me in my emotional journey. I'm so grateful to have expanded this way. Because of this new awareness, I am bringing my true, authentic self to the table, showing up for myself and others.

You will notice a subtitle under each chapter throughout my book. These are the wide range of emotions and feelings I had the great opportunity to feel over these last six months. I am so proud of myself for allowing all of them to come into my life, to sweep over my presence, to move through my body and then to leave. I am learning that life is at its best when these emotions can be fully felt. I am continuing to allow myself to fully feel all my emotions and then decide how long I want them to stay. It has been an amazing discovery for me.

At the end of each chapter is a gratitude statement. I have come to realize that it is important to have daily gratitude in my life. This keeps me grounded and reminds me that I have the ultimate choice in how I show up in life. So, I choose to connect to gratitude and remind myself that I have so many people, experiences, places (and so forth) to be grateful for.

Prologue

GRATITUDE THOUGHT: THANK YOU, SCOTT, FOR ALWAYS SHARING YOUR FEELINGS, THOUGHTS AND WHAT YOU ARE GOING THROUGH.

CHAPTER 1

August 2022

I AM PROUD, LOVED, JOYOUS, SCARED, EXCITED, NERVOUS, SAD

Five thousand kilometres across Canada

A few days after our wedding, Scott was all packed up for one of the longest rides he had ever been on. And for me, the longest bike ride *ever*! At that point, I had been on the motorcycle for a few hours at a time. I didn't really find that amount of time on the back of the Harley tiring; however, it was more about getting used to being a passenger and trusting the rider and all the other drivers on the road.

Scott started out on Tuesday, July 26, for his cross-Canada trip. He has proven that he is the Packing King. He can pack a bike for a long trip like no other. He was fully prepared and set off in the dark, on a wet Tuesday morning. Remember, we just got married on the 23rd of July, so it was hard to say goodbye for the next six days. I just married this man, and now I have to say goodbye for almost a week. *Ahhhh!* And I worried about him getting into an accident or having any major problems—although I knew he was a highly competent rider. Thank goodness for all the Wi-Fi stops along the way.

I don't remember why I didn't go with him on this west-to-east drive. Maybe we thought it was just too long for me. Maybe I had other commitments. Either way, the plan was made, and I would meet him in P.E.I. on August 1.

Scott had one big hiccup along his journey. Not being there when it happened, I don't know his immediate reaction; however, when he contacted me, he calmly told me, "I pulled out my phone while I was riding and put it in the cubby hole on the handlebar area. Well, it didn't stay there; something was in the way (a wallet or something). My cell phone went bouncing onto the wet pavement, and it was toast."

This is probably the biggest problem Scott encountered over his six days of travel. *Whew!* on my part. From home, I helped him find an Apple Store to purchase a new phone. After this hiccup, he continued his journey to the east.

He was getting close to Prince Edward Island, and I was so super excited for him. I kept my family abreast of his travels, and they were getting excited to meet him too. My whole family was going to P.E.I. that summer for a bit of a family reunion. Scott had already met my sister, Lana, and my mom, Eleanor. However, he would be meeting my dad and two brothers in person for the first time. To top it off, he would meet my dad for the first time without me. I was okay with that, as he met him online over our many Skype calls (which I talked about in *A Year of Love*).

August 2022

My dad, Peter, an avid scooter rider himself, was so excited to meet Scott. I think biking was the one thing they had in common—oh yeah, both were a little stubborn too! (Did I say that out loud?) Dad was already planning Scott's trip back to his house when Scott arrived on The Island after riding over the Confederation Bridge.

Dad was all ready to give up his bed to give Scott a good night's sleep after five days of travelling. While Scott vocalized very clearly that he would not kick a 78-year-old man out of his own bed, Dad was adamant that Scott would "come around" and take his bed while he would sleep on his living room floor. This created a whole new stress for Scott, and I knew at that point that I needed to step up for him. I spoke with Dad on several occasions that Scott *would not* be taking his bed and would sleep on the floor. I knew I needed to do my best to share Scott's feelings with Dad.

Scott met up with Dad at Tim Hortons on The Island and was surprised at how tiny in stature Dad was; he only saw Dad from the waist up on our biweekly Skype calls. Even though Dad could be as stubborn as Scott, his presence was probably less intimidating.

Dad and Scott had a little bit of a rough start. Scott felt like Dad wasn't hearing him, and I believe that Dad was just trying to be a good host. However, you looked at it, it was a rough start, but I believe Scott's clarity in what he wanted was clear to Dad, whether he liked it or not. Dad rarely encounters someone like Scott—someone so sure about what he wants and needs to be heard. Scott knew where he stood with his elders; on top of that, this was his new wife's dad, and he would not take his bed.

Scott's certainty in what he wants and needs is one thing I love about him. There are no wishy-washy thoughts. I see how he has needed to be this way. He has learned to stick his heels in and be the bull in the china store to be heard and not be walked over.

I found myself a little stressed over the situation. Should Scott have been more flexible, as Dad was being kind and offering his bed? On the other hand, Scott won't ask his new 78-year-old father-in-law to sleep on the floor. I could see both points of view. I knew that they needed to work it out, not me. In the end, Scott slept on the living room floor, and Dad kept his bed.

Dad left early the next day, and Scott woke up to an empty house. I know it wasn't a smooth start to their first meeting; however, I think it worked out and how it happened was meant to happen.

I believe Dad wasn't 100 percent sure about Scott, as he came across as a vocal, strong man who needed to be heard and knew what he wanted. Also, Scott's tattooed arms, gruff voice and solid physique could be intimidating, for sure. Sometimes we meet people who challenge us and our thinking. I feel that's what Scott did for Dad. I know that's what Scott does for me. When Scott came into my life, he was a wake-up call for me. He woke me up to being heard, making decisions, having an opinion and being okay with being strong and vulnerable at the same time.

The reunion

My flight plan was to fly from Calgary to Toronto and then finally to P.E.I. I organized a flight from Toronto to Charlottetown with my older brother, Darren, his wife, Vanessa, and their two kids. It was so great to see and spend time with them (even if it was just in the airport). Covid has kept us apart for about three years now.

On the plane, I was getting so excited to be able to see Scott again. I wanted to hold him, kiss him and just be in his presence again. He's been on the road for about a week now, and I just needed to have him

August 2022

in my arms. It was also on this flight that I decided to see if I could write a book about Scott—at least, that's what I thought the book's focus would be. I started to type my thoughts into the Notes app on my phone. As I wrote, I scrolled to the top to write the title, *Why Scott?*

The words seemed to pour out of me pretty easily; however, I was finding it difficult to add enough content to think I would ever write at least 25,000 words. Well, I was proud of what I started with—so proud that I took my phone to Darren and asked him to read the start of my very first book and give me some feedback. He said it was good. And that was my humble beginning to writing my first book, *A Year of Love*. With Darren's thoughtful nod, I thought I could really do this. Thanks, Darren. I appreciate your words that day.

The five of us arrived in Charlottetown and were greeted by Mom, Dad, Lana, my brother Dean, his wife, Yvonne, and their kids—Carter and Gavin. And, of course, Scott, who greeted me with a bouquet of roses; really, all I wanted was him. I was filled with such joy, love and bliss to hold and kiss him.

If you have seen the front cover of *A Year of Love*, there is something you need to know. That picture wasn't taken in the year I wrote about. That picture was taken by Dad, the once-upon-a-time wedding photographer, when I arrived at the airport. It was such a great shot that I decided to use it as the cover for the book. I couldn't resist using that picture, even though it was just outside the actual "year of love." I love that photo so much because I feel the love between us. I loved that all my family could see the love I felt for Scott, and I was so excited for him to spend time with my family—now his family.

The last time we were all together in P.E.I. was in the summer of 2019. It felt so good to hold and hug everyone again. The stress and strain of Covid restrictions have reinforced that having one-to-one time with my family is precious. In P.E.I., we toured around, tested out the local food (always the best fish and chips) and met the locals. Scott and I rented a house within walking distance of Mom's, Lana's and Darren's accommodations. Dean was about a ten-minute drive away, as his wife had family on The Island. Dad also lived about ten minutes away.

Scott knew my family fairly well at this point. He was part of our family Skype calls, has met with Lana on many occasions and took care of my mom when she came to Calgary and unfortunately broke her elbow. Scott looked after my mom during the previous spring.

Darren seemed to like Scott. He was often more vocal than the rest of our family and not afraid to share it. Scott and Darren jived, and it was great to see. Scott also got to meet my younger brother, Dean—a very relaxed kind of guy who doesn't get too stressed over much. He appeared to be happy with being around Scott.

It was so great to have my family accept Scott. They had fun including him in conversations and had a blast with activities we did, such as cornhole and deep-sea fishing. We also had a backyard family BBQ, where we shared old photos and stories of growing up. I was blessed to see my family include Scott and show him love and acceptance.

Our family also had many dining-out experiences. One memorable dinner out for Scott and me was when we had to stand in line (with some spitting rain) for almost an hour and a half for P.E.I.'s traditional lobster dinner at the New Glasgow Lobster Suppers. Scott was excited, and so was I. I love lobster! After the long wait, we each ordered two lobsters (a one-and-a-half-pound lobster and an additional one-pound lobster for a special price). I was excited to share my knowledge of how and what parts to eat. I worked in lobster restaurants almost every summer during my late teenage years. What a fun but stinky job—I always went home smelling like lobster.

When we sat down to our lobster dinner, we got the salad, soup and delicious buns. And then the lobster. Scott still tells this story about how I was done with my two lobsters well before he was done with his first. I guess it pays to know the skill of eating a lobster.

Another one of the most memorable parts of summer was watching Scott let loose and just be playful with Darren's twins—Jack and Aimee. Scott discovered they brought some tennis balls to play with during their vacation. It was an opportunity to have some fun, and Scott sure did. He played monkey in the middle with the twins and, at one point, "stole" a ball. We took pictures of the tennis ball that had been "stolen" and found it in a bag of avocados. It was a lot of fun joking around with Jack and Aimee, and it filled my heart to see Scott play, laugh and be carefree. I had only seen him this "carefree" with his two younger cousins on our trip down to Seattle back in June. It's beautiful to watch when I know he carried a heavy emotional load from his past. I know Scott can be judged from the outside—big guy with a bunch of tattoos. However, when the playful guy comes out, it's great for everyone, including him.

The great road trip

Our time in P.E.I. came to an end on August 14. I was mentally gearing up to travel for our big road trip, wherein I would spend three to ten hours daily on the back of a Harley for almost two weeks.

On the Cabot Trail in Nova Scotia, Canada

Scott had a rough idea of how we would get back to Calgary, about 5,000 km away, on the bike. We would stop at his hometown in Ontario and I would meet his Alcoholics Anonymous (AA) mom, Phyllis, in person for the first time.

I was so grateful to finally meet his mom—the lady who truly believed in him and backed him for all these years of sobriety and through his earlier struggles. Phyllis and I both deeply care for Scott and only want the best for him. Thank you, Phyllis, for being Scott's rock in his life.

August 2022

Phyllis And Scott

Some things that I learned over this year came into play for this biking trip. I've grown through many things and gained much clarity when dealing with challenges. I had 100 percent trust in the rider of this bike and where he and I were going. He knew where I came from—I was learning to be a passenger on the back, and he made it a priority to check in with me. I also found myself open to finding a hotel at the end of each day—and did we find some interesting places to sleep in! It was all good. It was an adventure.

At one point on our journey in the States, a state trooper pulled us over. We were going about 10 km over the speed limit. All I was thinking was, *Oh my, this officer is going to have one look at my hubby and slap us with a fine.*

When he approached us, Scott handed him his license and registration, and the officer returned to his state trooper car.

I realized then that I had a choice: Get all worried, see the fine we were about to receive and see ourselves upset. Or I could see the officer giving us a simple warning and be on our way. I chose to switch my mind and believe what I wanted. I chose to remind myself then that Scott was doing his best to get us back to Calgary, safe and sound. We were just a recently married couple, in love and enjoying our honeymoon trip. I saw the officer as someone who sees us as a loving couple who just made the simple mistake of going too fast, and we would only receive a warning.

After sitting in the hot sun in our bike gear and sweating it out, the officer returned to us and said, "This is a warning. Watch your speed."

My positive thoughts worked that day! No fine. All good, and we were well on our way.

We made it back to Calgary on August 25. The first thing on my mind? Have a nice long shower and properly wash some clothes. And, of course, be oh-so grateful for my husband's riding skills and getting us home safely to my kids. Brianna was at home and, of course, I took a selfie with all of us together. Yes, babe. I know it's not technically a selfie.

August 2022

Made it home to Calgary, Alberta

A new home

A major event was coming up for us—our trip to Thailand. We were packing up our Calgary home, so we could rent it out while we were away. Here was another transition, another change. How do I choose to handle it? I spent time and money buying things for my house, choosing where I wanted each to go and how to set it all up the way I wanted it. Many items in our home were already sold before I went on the bike trip with Scott, and Brianna sold off more items while I was away.

I was now looking at my bed, which I had chosen a few months before moving into my new home, after my first husband and I separated. Choosing my bed was a monumental thing for me. It was not only a higher-priced purchase as a "single woman" but a representation of me moving forward and choosing what I wanted and the bed I would sleep in for the rest of my life. Isn't it interesting how we attach stories and realizations to material possessions? Now there I was, saying goodbye to my bed and that milestone and being okay with that. I was learning to make these grievances more quickly. When I sat in reflection, I asked myself, *What were "things"?* They are just energy. My bed was a tangible representation of my energy and confidence to move my life forward and love myself.

We asked Scott's friends, Mark and Mike, to support us in moving to Ashcroft, B.C. They arrived with Mark's truck pulling a rented trailer to pack all our things into. At that point, I was beginning to understand more about what real friends will do. Mark and Mike offered their time and strength to get all of our house's contents into the trailer and move it up to B.C., which is seven hours away.

There was a bonus for Scott, though—one I know he appreciated and enjoyed. As Mark and I, along with the two dogs, Norton and Alya, rode in the truck pulling the heavy trailer, Mike and Scott zoomed up together on their Harleys—Scott's place of freedom. I was glad he was enjoying the time with his friend, and I looked at this as a way to get to know Mark a little more. The doggies settled in for the long ride on the back seat and kept each other company.

As we approached Ashcroft, I realized I was almost at my new home—a new experience, a new adventure. What would living in Scott's home along with his buddy Mark be like?

I knew Scott loved the quiet town of Ashcroft, away from the chaos of the city. He could discover new people who didn't know about his past and make relationships without the past coming back to haunt him. This is, of course, how I saw it. It was a fresh start, in some way. He has told me that people, in his past, have often referred to him as

August 2022

Angry Scott. Yet, when I met Scott last summer during the week of the Ranch, I did not see Angry Scott. I saw a man who was so raw and ready for love. I saw a man who deserved love. I still see him that way to this day. I'm not blind to his past; I'm just choosing to see the man he is confidently stepping into.

While this new start in Ashcroft gave Scott the opportunity to proactively chime in with new people without ties to his past, my goal was to get out and around town to meet people and talk to neighbours. I chose, almost daily, to take out the dogs for a walk, and they loved it. I discovered the town and had time to decompress and enjoy my space. I met Peter at the local museum, where I learned more about Ashcroft and its history. I also met a neighbour across the street who has lived here for several years—Yvonne, a kind Harley-riding woman.

Yvonne had invited Scott and me over to her house for breakfast, and we enjoyed her company. She was planning to sell her house and move back to Calgary to be close to her kids and grandkids. It was with a heavy heart to hear that Yvonne passed away while we were in Thailand. She had a beautiful way about her. She had moved back to Calgary while we were in Thailand, and she had a fun Christmas (according to her FB posts) with her grandkids. Scott and I will miss her.

GRATITUDE THOUGHT: I AM GRATEFUL FOR HOW AWARE I AM THAT I CONTINUE TO BE A STUDENT. TO BE OPEN TO LEARN AND ACCEPT FAILURE, AND LOOK AT IT AS AN OPPORTUNITY FOR GROWTH.

CHAPTER 2

September 2022

I AM PROUD, EXCITED, NOSTALGIC, INSPIRED, INCLUDED, CHERISHED

Sitting on the back deck of our home, which overlooked the little town and the incredible mountain range, I looked at my phone and noticed the date. It was the first day of school. With coffee in hand, I sat quietly. The back-to-school hustle and bustle was in the air. I heard children's voices, excited and nervous. I saw a mom walking her child down the street, with an excited dog pulling them along. I smelled the crisp air and heard the rustle of dried leaves falling off the trees.

My general leave of absence from my Calgary teaching job for the 2022–2023 school year just got approved, and I had a sense of nostalgia and a sense of loss. A loss for a routine that was my life for almost twenty years as a teacher and, of course, the seventeen years of schooling. I loved being a teacher.

I took this moment to reflect.

When I was packing up my classroom last July, on my way to a new adventure in Thailand and not knowing exactly what the future held, I was sad. Sad for closing a chapter of that routine. However, I hold all those memories dear to me. I am so grateful for all the positive feelings I feel when I think of school and all the connections I have to it.

I now see that life is not always best lived when in my comfortable spot. And my teaching profession was a comfortable spot. I remained a class teacher and never expanded my comfort zone to see what I was capable of. Maybe I never thought I was capable. I was still growing in my own skin.

September was also the month Brianna went off to college and stayed on campus, which was about an hour away from Calgary. It was a proud and sad moment for me. I was so proud of her for deciding to pursue a career working with animals, and yet sad that I was seeing my second (and last) baby grow up. I've watched her struggle and grow during her life, and I'm so proud that she is taking on this learning opportunity to be in charge of herself and her studies, make new friends, make sure she eats well and ask for support when she needs it. I was a proud Mama!

I decided to drive down to Calgary by myself and support her on her move into her dorm. I asked my son, Jordan, to join us, as we had several items to take down and I really wanted to spend time with both my kids. It was an absolutely beautiful experience! At one point, they were walking ahead of me, and their body language showed a sign of love and comfort with each other. I tear up to this day, thinking of how beautiful this was and how grateful I am that they have each other.

Those few days with my kids were so special to me. I've come to truly understand that it is up to me to let others know how much I truly love them. I realized how connections with people are extremely important and necessary.

Letting others know that you see and appreciate them is key and makes this world worth living in. So, before going back to Ashcroft, I stepped out of my comfort zone on purpose as I took the time to drop off a thank-you gift to a friend and co-worker, Krystal. While standing on her front porch, with no answer at the door, I sent her a quick video of how much I appreciated her and that it was too bad I missed her.

I did a quick turnaround, back to Ashcroft, having fun blasting my music and singing my tunes. Life is great!

Viva la Mexico

In mid-September, Scott and I took a week-long personal development course, called Momentum, before our big Thailand trip. We packed up the Rav4, and by September 10, we were getting email reminders about our upcoming event at the Eldorado Hotel in Santa Fe, New Mexico!

We were on a path in our lives where we're beginning to understand what we were capable of. We were excited to have coaches supporting and reminding us that our lives are meant to really be lived. We are meant to be confident beings. We *are* confident beings.

We drove to Calgary and met up with our friend Julie, who was performing her karaoke during the Calgary Stampede (one of the biggest outdoor shows in the world). It was fun watching her perform and then get white-hatted, a tradition recognized during Stampede. That day we received an email stating that our six-month visa was approved for Thailand. That was exciting news and another check off the list so that we can move forward.

After a 3-hour plane ride from Calgary to Santa Fe, we hopped on a shuttle that seemed unfamiliar with our hotel's location, as it drove around aimlessly. When we finally arrived, we found out that our hotel was about ten minutes away from the main hotel where most students were booked and the personal development (PD) activities were taking place. A feeling of being the "outsiders" crept in; we were not good enough just because we didn't book early, or maybe we weren't important enough. These thoughts were happening more with Scott than with me; I often choose to look on the bright side of situations, and he often had more difficulty with this skill.

While I watched Scott sit in that "poor me" space, I chose to pivot. I looked at it as an opportunity to get a walk in every day; maybe meet new people in the hotel or on the walk. I chose to take a different perspective. This is something we often talk about. His awareness of this challenge of looking at things differently was a recurring conversation. He knows that the time he spends on making this change in perspective has improved greatly over the last few years of PD work, and he knows it will become even better as he continues to grow. I support him on that journey, for sure. I've watched him swing these perspectives much quicker over the time I've been with him. It's been an amazing journey to watch and be part of.

A group activity that took place during Momentum was an encouraging event for Scott. I saw others listen to him and hear him. This was something that was not always easy for Scott. We were sent on a mission to build a cardboard boat and sail it down the river in competition with other groups. Scott, having run a business and having management experience, piped up and said he would like to be the *leader* of the boat-building competition with our group of six people.

I saw a confident, assertive Scott—hearing others give ideas on how to construct a boat and still being certain to share his knowledge of how a particular design will aid our success. I saw how he managed a space where many voices were speaking, and he found success. It was great to see my husband succeed and have it recognized by him and our group.

Like Scott, I also stepped forward in this boat-building activity and stretched my comfort zone. I chose to be one of the "dramatic" presenters to promote our boat as the ultimate floating design. I stood up with our groupmates, Ken and Laney, and gave it my all. I was nervous about doing such a thing, and I found myself just taking some more breaths and reminding myself to "Just do it"—or, as you learned in my last book, JFDI! Yes, the *F* is *fuckin'*. I love that I am able to recognize this and I am able to do something about it.

During this week-long transformation class in Santa Fe, we signed up for the biggest (and when I say biggest, I'm referring to money and time) course we had ever invested in. Scott and I were unstoppable and liked that we chose to move forward in our lives for our betterment as a couple and as individuals.

A big realization is not that we are discovering who we really are but letting go of who we think we are, all the doubts and all the feelings of unworthiness. We are creating daily goals, weekly goals and so forth to pull back the unwanted layers and discover who really is in there; not all the stories we've heard over the years nor the reinforcing of those stories we've heard. They are the past. They are not now. They are not me. They are not my future, because I choose to show me and not the old stories I have been told.

Saying hello, saying goodbye

The week-long course was over, and we flew back to Calgary. On September 18, we jumped into the Rav4 and headed back to Ashcroft to get ready for our next big lifestyle shift—the biggest ever!

Before heading to Thailand, we got to do one more biking adventure in Canada. We decided to make our way west to Vancouver to meet up with a few friends and a special lady that Scott has referred to as family, like a sister or mom, and a life-long friend—Colleen. We arranged to bring over some local fish and chips for dinner to share with Colleen and her five-year-old grandson, Dax. Colleen expressed how she saw such loving growth in Scott and was excited to meet me as well. Scott and I had fun conversing and playing around with Dax, and it was special meeting them both.

On our quick trip to Vancouver, I also connected with Kerry, an old neighbour who lived right across from my childhood house in P.E.I. It was great to connect with Kerry. His house was right next to my best friend, Sandra, who had flown to see me in Calgary back in April 2022. (You can read more about it in my first book, *A Year of Love*)

Back in Ashcroft, I needed some time with my biggest furball during my last few days in the country. I usually take Norton and Alya out for a walk together, although not on September 25. On that day, Alya and I ventured out on our last walk together, and I sat her down on a bench on our path.

September 2022

My last walk with Alya

On our last walk together, I spoke to her out loud. "I love you very much, Alya. I found you a loving home to stay at—a great friend's, Carrie—in Calgary. Scott and I are heading to Thailand. I would love to bring you, but it's too hot for you.

"I'm going to miss you so much. I will not forget you, and I want you to be the best doggie you can. You will love Carrie and her two boys. Brianna will make sure she drops in and takes you for walks. Also, I've made sure that Cody (Alya's dog walker) will still come to pick you up, so you can go walking with your friends. I love you so much, Alya."

I was really sad to say goodbye to Alya. I was going to miss her a great deal. She is a very loving dog who brought peace and happiness into my life, even with her sneaky personality.

The next day, Scott, Mark and I took Norton and Alya on a car ride to Calgary to introduce Alya to Carrie and her kids. After dropping Alya off, Scott and I got a hotel room with Norton, and Mark visited family in Calgary. This trip to Calgary was also our opportunity to have one last dinner with Brianna, Jordan and his girlfriend, Alannah. We met up with them at a local pub and enjoyed our last dinner together. Brianna, who especially took a shine to Norton, also got to say goodbye to her little buddy.

Our last family dinner before Thailand

It's so hard doing "lasts." They really make you think about how short life is and how much you need to make sure that people know how much you care and love them.

September 2022

By the 28th, Scott also said goodbye to his buddy Norton. Mark drove my Rav4 to the Calgary Airport, where Scott got in his last hugs with his dog. I could tell this was hard for Scott, although there were no tears. Norton has been his buddy for about eight years at that point. We were blessed to also have our great friend, Mark, help us out in this way. So, last hugs and goodbye to Mark too.

We got on the plane and off to Vancouver, then Tokyo, then Bangkok. After twenty-two hours of travel, we made it!

Thailand, here we come!

Arriving in Thailand

Thailand was a little test for us—figuring out how to manage together in a new country, new language, new money and so many unknowns. We were doing just fine, albeit with a few stressors that we acknowledged and got through. But first things first—get to our hotel and relax.

After arriving, we settled into our hotel, got a taxi to downtown Bangkok, toured some stunning temples and just took it all in as best we could. It was all a little surreal. We were really doing this; really taking on something this big (well, at least from my perspective).

I've been on many big trips during my previous marriage, and it wasn't about that. It was that I was shaking up my life—looking at making a career change and doing it all with the man who supported me in who I was and how I was shifting and growing. Wow! That was the surreal part.

We were slowly learning to use Google Translate to translate from English to Thai to ask for what we needed to eat—if we could get veggies and some protein, we were doing good. One thing we slowly learned: Don't forget to ask for *no spice*. For me, none is better; Scott did his best to get across the point of "just a little spice," gesturing with his pointer finger and thumb close together.

September 2022

GRATITUDE THOUGHT: I SIT IN THE KITCHEN AND LISTEN TO THE CONFIDENT AND EMPATHETIC SCOTT, TALKING TO A FRIEND—CARRIE. HE SMILES, LAUGHS AND IS BEING HEARD. IT'S A BEAUTIFUL THING. THANK YOU FOR ENRICHING MY LIFE WITH YOUR CONVERSATIONS WITH OTHERS.

CHAPTER 3

October 2022

I AM CALM, ENTHUSIASTIC, BLESSED, HUMBLED, CERTAIN

Hello, Hua Hin

After our few days in Bangkok, we made our way to Hua Hin, a three-and-a-half-hour cab ride down south. We were fortunate that Scott had a friend in Thailand—John, and his wife, Tiky. I had met John on some previous video calls with Scott when we were in Calgary. I looked forward to getting to know them more and exploring Thailand.

By October 2, we saw beautiful scenery and monkeys and rented our first scooter. We were enjoying the simplicity of a one-bedroom condo. I often found myself taking in the beautiful view from the fourth-level condo, which overlooked the town of Hua Hin.

Getting groceries at the local store was an interesting venture. I was slowly learning to Google translate ingredients on a container, as most labels were in Thai. However, if it was whole food, like vegetables and meat, we were good. We mostly stayed away from packaged food, although yogurt was where we struggled to read the containers using our camera and Google Translate. We did our best, and if our tummies suffered, we realized that it wasn't translated properly into English, and we'd choose a different yogurt.

Eating properly was one important thing for Scott and me. For me, it's because I have established healthy-eating habits over the last several years that contributed to a healthy weight and clearer mind. For Scott, diet was the way he controlled his diabetes. Eating more cleanly positively affected his mental health too. However, it's interesting how the bombardment of new things, like yummy-looking "treats," can easily sway you from your regular habits and routines. Yes, we often ate out and chose yummy local treats like Thai coconut pancakes, a discovery at the local night market.

The local night market proved to be an enjoyable place for a night out together. One local vendor, bearing more tattoos than Scott, displayed all the seafood his restaurant served, and we had a great chat with this guy over the many times we frequented this market. It was a little like seeing an old friend when we would see each other on our evening walk through the market.

We learned the local way of saying hello: *Sa-wa-dee-kaw* (as a female) and *Sa-wa-dee-krap* (as a male) while bowing and with palms pressed together. With this under our belts, many locals showed us a welcoming smile and a returned gesture.

As I was well aware of connecting with those I love, I watched Scott prioritize this in his life too. I found this inspirational. When we first arrived in the condo, I watched him engaged in the video phone call with his AA mom, Phyllis. As I watched his body language and his verbal expression, I saw how he appreciated her. I'm learning all the time from Scott. It's the person. It's the soul. It's the spirit that you need in your life. When I talk to my mom, I know I'm being heard, and I saw at that moment that Phyllis was that to him—being heard and having a soft place to land. It was beautiful to see.

* * *

When we arrived in the one-bedroom condo with the large swimming pool at our disposal, I decided I needed a goal for myself. I knew I would be scuba diving at some point while we were here in Thailand, and I was mentally preparing for my level of comfort under the water. I've always loved swimming; however, I could never go underwater without closing my nose with a nose clip or my fingers. I now had all the time in the world to work on this.

I practiced and practiced and kept my positive mindset at the forefront. I was feeling very grateful for this experience, and I was having success! I gained confidence and extended the time I was able to stay underwater without holding my nose. My mind is really amazing!

Scott, too, was determined to set some new goals for himself: To work on his physical health. After a few times in the pool, he created a goal of achieving thirty lengths of the pool by the end of the month. He was bound and determined, even with the body pain he faced. He did it! His body suffered after this, and he decided to break away from this major physical push. When we decided to move on from this condo with the large pool, we found accommodations with a pool that we used more for relaxation than a workout.

The condo complex had a main entrance with a guard that let you in and out twenty-four seven. Just outside was an old storefront that was no longer occupied. On our way in one day, we saw a few adorable pups and their mama. If you know anything about Thailand, stray dogs or even owned dogs wander around everywhere in the streets. We had come to understand that this particular mom and her pups were there because the owner probably could not afford to keep her anymore, along with those new mouths to feed. Scott, of course, would stop and get off the bike whenever we saw them and give them some TLC. He even made it a point to put dog treats on the grocery list and would stop and give them some treats.

On the last few days of October, we saw several other people hovering around the mom. They said it looked like she had been hit by a car, and they were calling someone to get her and the pups to the vet. The next day, the mom and her pups were no longer out at the empty storefront, but I was left with a positive memory. I was appreciative that Scott chose to stop and see those cute doggies and let them know someone cared. I love how he shows me such love and care for other living things. It's this kind of care and thoughtfulness I want in my life. I am grateful that I get to see such love.

Officially Lisa Brearley

You may remember from my first book that Scott had the same birthdate as my son. For his birthday, our new friends suggested a local restaurant on the beach. It was a beautiful place, and we were the only ones in the restaurant. I was so proud to celebrate with my man and our new friends.

October 2022

The big day arrived! Back in Ashcroft, our marriage certificate came in the mail! Our friend Mark opened our mail for us and sent a pic of the certificate. Finally, a legal confirmation of our marriage.

What a nice surprise that was! It was official. When I get back home to Canada, I have a long list of things that need to be changed, like credit cards, passport and so forth. I also started changing my social media to Lisa Dawn Brearley. You see, my Facebook was Lisa Dawn for the longest time. Why, you ask? Since I was a teacher, I really didn't want or need all my students and their parents looking me up and seeing all that I was doing. I had the stance that they didn't need to know my business.

It wasn't until I had more confidence in myself and my posts that I felt I no longer needed to 'hide.' I decided that I wanted more people to see what I was doing. I was proud of who I was becoming and what I was doing. However, for those who knew me on FB as Lisa Dawn, I just added the Brearley so that I could be found.

Mr. and Mrs. New Skills

I was cruising around Facebook one day and came across a book writing program about getting support with writing your book and getting it published. Was the universe talking to me? Was this a sign? I enquired with Natasa Denman, a fourteen-book published author and creator of the business The Ultimate 48 Hour Author, who was offering a free info session. So I said, "What the heck?"

Next thing I knew, I was signed up to write my first book, *A Year of Love*, attended an author's writing retreat online in November and was scheduled to publish my book by March 15, 2023—what a great birthday present!

It was a financial commitment, and so I was committed. I felt a sense of invigoration and purpose here in Thailand. I was excited to venture out on this new limb and learn new skills—writing and sharing my story.

Typing the book came fairly easy. The words flowed, and having a phone full of pictures helped to recall all the fantastic memories from August 15, 2021 to July 23, 2022. That "year" has been one of the most amazing journeys of my life. Stretching my comfort zone to having my soulmate, Scott, has been the most beautiful combination this woman has needed in her life.

I found myself setting large blocks of time sitting on the condo deck and just typing. It was therapeutic, as I was so grateful for the work I have done on myself and how I have learned to show up in this beautiful relationship with my husband. Writing was an area I felt confident in. I was educated as a teacher and taught for almost twenty years. The realization that I could *become* an author was just within my reach; I just had to put in the time and effort and be open to learning and receiving constructive criticism.

Meanwhile, Scott signed up for a workshop on wealth. This was an area both he and I needed to look at. Scott took the initiative on this course, as it was presented online and started around 10 p.m. (Thailand time) and ended early in the morning. He made it a priority to stay up all night. I was not able to do so; I found myself nodding off. However, he was able to push through, and I'm very proud of him for doing so.

It was a great awareness for us. Overall, we did okay and needed to acknowledge that we have done well in our life. At this point, we needed to keep better tabs on our spending and budget. This is still something we both continue to work on.

October 2022

The spasms are back

In *A Year of Love*, I wrote about the spasms I had with my left foot and hand and that shortly after letting my former husband know I needed to move on from our marriage, these spasms subsided. I came to an understanding that stress was coming out of my body like I never thought possible at the time. Well, they're back. I was experiencing this again. However, because I had clarity on this, I knew what the stressor was this time.

I was stressing over being on the back of a little scooter in a new country, riding on the other side of the road and not feeling in control. But now that I have the awareness and tools to understand what was happening on my left side, I could emotionally and physically do something about it.

I took control in a few ways. I talked about it with Scott and had several appointments with an osteopath in Hua Hin. Next, I chose to keep my body active and moving. I was also more conscious about the way I kept my posture on the bike. I made it known that I needed breaks from any long riding excursions that we took. All these helped to reduce the left-side annoyance.

Eating in Thailand

Along with doing our best to support the local economy, we chose to shop mostly from local Thai vendors at the open market every day. The markets were full of fresh veggies, fruit, meat and eggs. The last two sure surprised us at first. We were shown that eggs did not need to be refrigerated, so we always left them on our dining table. We had no issues. As for the meat, we didn't leave it out on the table—that's disgusting. However, we bought the meat just sitting out on the table at the market. We requested the amount we wanted, they weighed it on the scale and put it in a baggie, we paid, and off we went. This meat always had to be consumed within a few days of purchasing it, yet we found it much more flavourful than what we ate in Canada.

Two things that we saw often had me in a place of bewilderment. For one, they use a lot of plastic baggies—for veggies, meat, drinks and seemingly everything. Second, the price for all that food we bought at the market was so much cheaper, and often tastier, than what we got back home in Canada. We also discovered that eating out is much cheaper than in Canada. We have gone for cheap meals that cost us THB 200 and others that cost THB 1,000. An expensive meal was around CAN$40. We were excited that meals were this cheap because it meant we could go out and try new food and interact with more locals.

One restaurant that we were introduced to was an all-you-can-eat BBQ. When it's an all-you-can-eat, sometimes the quality is poor, but not this place. Everything is high quality—from prawns to various meat to fish to lots of veggies. Best of all, it is cheap too. Getting as stuffed as you can costs THB 250—that's about CAN$10!

I always chose to eat a lot of veggies and protein. I always walked away feeling great about my choices, and it didn't matter that it was cheap. All I knew was that it jived with what made me feel great! And that was important.

On the Island of Koh Tao

We bought a train ticket to head down to Champion, a southern Thai province, where we got a ferry ride to the island of Koh Tao. As we waited for the train to arrive in Hua Hin, I introduced myself to a young couple that appeared to be making a trek as backpackers. We chatted for a good twenty minutes and exchanged WhatsApp links. It is pretty cool opening up and getting to know others. I'm loving this newfound level of confidence I am seeing in myself.

On the island of Koh Tao, I treated Scott and myself to a hotel room that was so beautiful and romantic. The room we stayed in was called The Beach House. Through the French doors, we can see the Gulf of Thailand and breathe in the fresh air. It was an amazing stay, and we deserved it. It was the honeymoon we never got after we married—ha ha! We joke that we are on our honeymoon every day, and that's the way it should be.

Even though this was a beautiful and relaxing space, we also received a piece of very upsetting news. Scott had a phone call with a specialist that had performed a prostate-specific antigen (PSA) test on him before leaving for Thailand, and she needed to speak with him regarding the results. I didn't know anything about PSA levels and what it had to do with cancer or cancer returning. I later looked up more information on what it meant if PSA was detected again in the blood.

Prostate-specific antigen, or PSA, is a protein produced by normal, as well as malignant, cells of the prostate gland. The PSA test measures the level of PSA in the blood. For this test, a blood sample is sent to a laboratory for analysis. The results are usually reported as nanograms of PSA per milliliter (ng/mL) of blood.

> The blood level of PSA is often elevated in people with prostate cancer, and the PSA test was originally approved by the FDA in 1986 to monitor the progression of prostate cancer in men who had already been diagnosed with the disease. In 1994, FDA approved the PSA test to be used in conjunction with a digital

rectal exam (DRE) to aid in the detection of prostate cancer in men 50 years and older. Until about 2008, many doctors and professional organizations had encouraged yearly PSA screening for prostate cancer beginning at age 50. ("Prostate-Specific Antigen (PSA) Test," National Cancer Institute, https://www.cancer.gov/types/prostate/psa-fact-sheet#what-is-the-psa-test)

We woke up at some crazy hour to connect with the specialist and hear what she had to update Scott about. She said his PSA levels were detectable again, which Scott equated to his cancer returning. I had never been in such a situation before, and all I wanted to do was say, "I'm so sorry, Scott," as if this was some death sentence and the PSA levels would continue to rise, as Scott later declared to a few people with the news: "My cancer is back."

I did some research and learned a few things. PSA numbers and the fact that Scott had his prostate removed in a radical prostatectomy several years ago didn't really compute for him or me. This confused us; how can these prostate levels be detectable if there is no prostate?

With all the sense of doom and gloom, I was left questioning, "What do I do?" I've never supported someone in this headspace where they feel like they received a death sentence and that's the end. I knew I needed to go back to what we knew about our relationship; to be open and honest and tell how we are feeling. So, after just one "I'm sorry about this news, Scott," there was what felt like—to me—a long moment of silence.

Scott was also not very emotional in terms of wanting hugs when he needed some sort of physical space, some space to breathe after this news. I stayed close to him, held his hand and let the news get absorbed and fall to the floor. Then I said, in my "updated" version of being as open as possible, "Babe, I don't know what to say. I've never been in a situation like this."

"I know. I've never been here either, and I don't know what to say," Scott replied.

With that, we both knew we were there for each other, no matter what. No matter the battle, no matter how challenging life can get.

New friends

We returned to Hua Hin and enjoyed more great times with our new friends John, Tiky, Terry, Nam, Bob and his wife Nok over the month we have been here. I've been posting our adventures and new understandings of Thai culture and appreciating all the memories we were making.

We were invited to come and see Terry perform in a local restaurant bar. It's pretty normal in Thailand to have local restaurants with only three walls to the building, with its frontside usually wide open. However, this particular place was wide open in the front and back, behind the band.

Terry sang and played guitar with his Bamboo Heart Band. He's an interesting guy and knows a lot of things. He is married to the beautiful Nam, and they reside in Hua Hin too.

One bedroom won't cut it

Scott and I had a stressful day one day in the condo. Maybe it was due to the small space we were living in. Maybe we were missing familiarity. Maybe we just needed some space from each other. Whatever it was, we found ourselves at odds with each other.

At one point, Scott was getting frustrated about our conversation (which I don't even remember what it was about). He stormed out of the door and said he would be back later. He literally walked down the hall and returned. We came to an understanding that this unease and feeling of uncertainty in solving it was just going to be there. We would look at "it"—whatever "it" was—again and let ourselves be close to each other in the one-bedroom condo and just let it be. And that was okay with us.

All day, "it" was just there. Neutral energy was put into "it." We ate during the day, did our daily little jobs of computer work, relaxed, ate and so forth. "It" was just there. When evening came, we had time to let "it" dissipate. It no longer had energy. We were able to find loving space for each other again. We sat together and knew we loved each other even when uncomfortable things came up. We discussed our feelings and how this rough patch was just that—an understanding that growth and relearning about ourselves will have rough patches. It is up to us to respect each other and find a place to communicate at a loving level. We did, and our life resumed, and we grew from this experience.

We share this story with others as "The day we were at odds with each other" like it was monumental. We say this with certainty for two reasons: We were not really at odds; however, it was a rough day in our relationship. It's also amazing that we can look back and see that we understand we will work it out.

Just before the end of the month, we decided we needed a bigger space. We needed a little more physical space to chill out and have our respective personal spaces. Often, Scott would wake up earlier than I and need a place to go, but the condo didn't have much choice. Other times, we'd be on a Zoom call and wouldn't have a place to go. Also, we would have Brianna and Jordan coming at Christmas, and we were not excited to spend a bunch of money on hotel accommodations, which we'd have to travel to, as the condo wasn't near the hotel area. So, we decided to look at other accommodations that would suit us better.

Scott took it upon himself to enquire about some local house rentals. He found one that looked interesting and was originally posted for THB 25,000 (that's just over CAN$1,000) per month, but the ad for the rental stated that if we signed a contract to rent for six months, we would get the reduced price of THB 23,000 (just over CAN$800) per month. We were delighted with this house, which had three bedrooms, an easy-care yard, three king-size beds, laundry, a private yard, a pool table and, best of all, our own pool!

We met with the realtor, her daughter, and the owner of the house, Noi. The realtor's daughter was great at translating any Thai and English that was difficult for any of us. We requested THB 23,000 for the five months we hoped to stay, and it was a deal! Noi agreed, and we were excited about the move.

After a few days in the new rental, we found a few hiccups that were not apparent when we first looked at the house. The low counters in the kitchen made washing dishes even too challenging for me, so we ended up washing our dishes in the bathroom adjacent to the kitchen. As well, we needed to boil water to wash the dishes, which we got used to pretty quickly. Another new habit was to turn the propane tank on and off to light our stove every time we cooked.

Oh, the new routines were established quickly, and we loved our simpler way of living!

GRATITUDE THOUGHT: SOMETIMES YOU THINK YOU'VE HAD THE BEST ORGASM EVER, AND THEN YOU HAVE THE BEST ORGASM EVER. CAN I LEAVE IT AT THAT?

CHAPTER 4

November 2022

I AM GUILTY, OVERWHELMED, MOTIVATED, REASSURED, SURPRISED, SADDENED, LOST, WELCOMED

During our stay in Thailand, I often thought of Alya. I felt guilty for leaving her. I felt uneasy when a situation arose, like finding a place for her to stay when my friend Carrie was away, as I felt disconnected in terms of distance, making it stressful for me.

I needed to step up.

I came to the understanding, too, that we were liking it here in Thailand, which raised the question of what I would do with Alya. I had asked Carrie to take her while we were in Thailand (at least until the spring of 2023), and now I need to step up and tell her that our plans may change.

I was nervous and terrified to tell her, thinking she would be upset. So, on a phone call, I told her we love it here and asked what the chance would be of her keeping Alya. She told me that she and her kids quite love Alya, and the conversation remained open to the idea, although no decision was made.

The seed was planted.

Our new space

When we moved into our new rental, it was a beautiful space and every time we drove out of our home, we were greeted (or watched, depending on how you look at it) by the dogs on the street. Did they exactly belong to someone? We were not sure. However, they were looked after in some manner. As the month went by, we noticed a lady who parked her scooter near the dogs and divided up food for several of them to eat. That was amazing to see!

We were beginning to enjoy the tranquil space; however, the dog conversations on the streets during the night sometimes made our sleep challenging. The dogs were either having a party out there or yelling at their posse to get out of their space. Either way, putting those yelps and barks as part of our background noise in our new space was a little difficult.

Our new home was also quite a contrast to our previous accommodation. When we were on the fourth floor of the one-bedroom concrete condo building, life was pretty clean and easy. Not at our three-bedroom house rental, though. I was up one morning, getting a coffee mug for my first morning coffee, and I put the light on before entering the bathroom (if you remember, the counter was a lot higher for washing dishes). I picked up the large frying pan on top of the rest of the dishes, and there it was—a one-and-a-half-inch cockroach scurrying across the dish rack!

I quickly dropped the pan and ran out of the room. I'm not sure where I found the courage to go back in; however, I was recording all the new adventures I was going through here in Thailand and here was one. I got out my phone, lifted the pan again and got a shot of it. Eww!

Other than those, we loved our space in our new rental. We had the freedom to walk around the house naked if we wanted to or go skinny-dipping in the pool, as a solid fence surrounded the house. The pool was downtime for us for the most part. It's where I loved having conversations about our day, sharing about our challenges, celebrating our wins, enjoying each other's love and respect and being with each other.

The hot weather also made the pool an enjoyable way to exercise and work out my legs and butt muscles. Working out in the pool was good for my crappy left kneecap that haunts me occasionally. You see, when I was in Grade 9, I popped out my kneecap. It was an unusual experience. I sat down on the school bus seat and—with that act of turning and sitting, and the bus propelling forward to continue the route—out popped the kneecap. Because the kneecap was not popped in for several hours, it's now a bum knee and has altered how I operated in my physical activity all my life. So, let's just say the pool is a great spot to work out when you feel limited by the stress and strain you put on your body.

I loved the simplicity of the laundry situation too. Our laundry machine is outside, at the back of the house. There's no dryer, which I believe is very typical of Thailand, as it's much cheaper to hang your clothes out to dry—and with the heat, it was like, "*Ta-da*! It's dry."

Sometimes there were cross breeze winds that helped dry the clothes too. We only had to fish out a dish towel and a bed sheet out of the pool once. (Lesson learned!)

These new habits and routines made me realize that I do love the simplicity of life here and how this in itself is so abundantly beautiful. I am now more grateful for the time and space I've established here. I have come to realize that it's in these small things that I see beauty. It is important to me to take the time to just "be" and enjoy what I have and be grateful.

We also had a pool table outside. This was a great pastime for us. Well, Scott might say differently, as his experience and confidence in the sport were a little different than mine. I grew up with a pool table in my basement, and we played quite often. One of my most vibrant memories of the family pool table was with my older brother, Darren. I remember (and this memory may be skewed or only happened once, for all I know) that when we played, Darren would start the game with his turn. I would shoot next (maybe getting a ball in), and then Darren would go again, clearing the table and winning.

That probably didn't happen as much as I remember; however, it was a time to take some pointers as he kicked my ass (which felt like every time).

Well, now playing pool with Scott, a lot of those little tips and tricks (and the style of offensive and defensive thinking I saw my brother use) were all coming back. I was a little rusty; however, I felt pretty confident in my pool skills when I played with Scott. However, it wasn't always as fun. Scott often felt frustrated, whether it was because of something going on in his life that distracted him or that his skills were a little rusty. Whatever was happening with him, I was aware and allowed him space to process. When I was aware Scott was feeling impacted by uncertainty or whatever challenge, I strived to see how I could support him and jump on a new or different path of thinking.

I had also enquired with our trauma therapist, Kimberly, regarding how I can support Scott when going through lows and depression or maybe just that old self-doubt (what I have known so well). She suggested redirecting the brain with easy, simple questions like *What colour is your shoe? Which pool cue is longer? Where is the light switch?* This activates the brain with answers that the person knows, boosting their confidence and redirecting their thinking. I never became very good at this, although I think the method would be beneficial. I still strive to support my amazing husband when times are tough.

During this time, I realized it was important to share my journey with the world via social media, like Facebook, and see that if little old me could do it, anyone could do it. I had a second motive for posting about our journey in Thailand on Facebook. I know that I often beat myself up with my lack of remembering events, so these posts would resurface again in the future, helping to recall the amazing events in my life.

I also found that making posts meant that what I had to share was important. By creating posts and doing lives, I knew I would be heard by someone—even by at least one person. They may feel inspired. They may connect. They may see their own potential through me. It's a win-win, for sure.

Ultimate 48 Hour Author

I started looking at our three-bedroom space with purpose. I was now really focussed on writing my book, and my upcoming online author retreat was soon to happen in November. So, I organized one of the spare bedrooms as my office. It worked out great, and thank goodness for air conditioning!

I realized that becoming an author was twofold for me. I loved the creativity of sharing and writing; it empowered my life. The other was that I needed to watch the seclusion that came with this new passion of mine. Writing meant hours of quiet time by myself, tucked away in a room. I loved the quiet adult time (unlike my previous job as an elementary school teacher), yet being "locked up in a room" meant not having as much free time and space to spend with my husband.

I heard from him, on a few occasions, how I was always busy working in my office. Because of all the work I've done on myself and the conscious awareness I've learned, this comment meant we needed a conversation. I asked him how he was feeling, and he shared how he felt.

After our conversation, I looked at my time differently and took breaks to spend more valuable time with him. I took breaks to check in, say hi and give a kiss; then I'd return to work. We have learned that really hearing each other communicate is so key to having our relationship work.

Besides checking in with my love, I noticed I also needed my own mental breaks, which I incorporated too—taking time for music, breathing, meditation and just getting out for a coffee with my husband. Balance is so important, even with the understanding that all this work is for our future and this big shift that I am (we are) doing in my life.

On November 8, I was both excited and so nervous. I started the Ultimate 48 Hour Author retreat for my first book, *A Year of Love*. Well, no turning back now. I worked with other authors and my coach, Natasa Denman. She started the retreat by showing us our mock-up covers of the books we were writing, then we told a little about ourselves.

Again, I felt that my book, or at least what I have to say, is not that important. What is the real purpose of my book? Will it be perceived well? Will it be bought? Will it sound okay? I had so many questions filled with fear and uncertainty.

During the whole retreat, I felt uncertain about how I would share my first book. Several participants had a business that was part of their book release, so the book would draw people to their business, such as coaching or a program they offered.

Not me.

"What was my *why*?" I asked over and over again. I struggled with feeling confident in answering this question. However, through the coaching at the retreat, I became closer and closer to the answer. I wanted to feel confident in sharing my thoughts and feelings and, with this, inspire others about their own growth. Through my story, my readers can see how a healthy relationship of love and respect is possible in a second marriage.

This three-day online retreat lasted about eight hours each day, which meant a lot of time on the computer. I was up each morning at 4 a.m., and I was truly blessed to be 100 percent supported by Scott in my journey. He would cook breakfast and bring it to me, make me coffee and check in to see how it was going. Scott truly is a kind, caring soul.

Six Months Of Love

Settling down in Thailand

Now that we have gotten over the initial excitement of being here in Thailand and testing out new food we see, I have been able to settle down with my diet and get some consistency. You see, Scott manages his diabetes with food, and I have been learning about gut health and the importance of what goes in my body for about four years now.

I've noticed about myself (*again*) that I'm only human too—I need to be gentle with myself—and was putting on a few pounds the first month we arrived, testing out Thai coconut pancakes, Thai dishes with noodles and shrimp cakes dipped in a sweet sauce. They were all so delicious; however, they were not serving my body or brain.

As we got into a routine, our diet improved. We bought an air fryer and ate way more salads. I feel so much more incredible when I am able to do this. When I choose better things for myself, like with eating, physical activity and communicating clearly, other things seem to fall into play.

* * *

You may remember that my family has had Skype calls every other Sunday since Covid. Since being here in Thailand, a time change happened, and it was becoming very late for me to connect with everyone. I wrote an email and proposed a new time, so I would not have to be up at 11 p.m. I wrote everyone's new schedule, and they were all good with that.

I really am learning to speak up for myself and ask for what I want. This may seem so minor to you; however, as someone scared to feel confident in her thoughts or opinions, this is big for me.

* * *

November 2022

We took in some fantastic restaurants and Thai celebrations. One such celebration was Loy Krathong. This "festival of lights" saw us purchasing small homemade floating centrepieces, which we released into a body of water to take away misfortunes and start fresh with a clearer mind and enlightened soul.

I was blessed to see how Nam and Tiky (both native Thais) took the time to be present in the celebration and reflect on peace, joy and well wishes for their family and friends. I am so appreciative that I got to observe my new friends and that I was also able to participate in this Thai tradition. I appreciate taking the time to reflect on life and feel the gratitude that comes with that reflection.

Goodbye, Uncle Joe

November was also a tough month. Scott lost a blood relative, whom I believe he related very well with. We got word from Scott's Aunt Sandra that while we were on an adventure in the southern part of Thailand, Uncle Joe took a turn for the worse and was hospitalized during their Mexican vacation. They were running some tests, and we would be updated when they returned to Canada.

Upon his return to Canada, the doctors gave Joe a limited time to live. I really struggled with this. I knew Scott's connection with his family was limited, and this was one really important link he had to his family. Scott admired how Joe turned his life around and how he had success in his life.

I supported Scott with whatever decision he wanted to make about seeing Joe or what he needed to do in this situation. We were on a trip to Phuket, Phi Phi and Krabi when we found out Joe passed away. I have never really been in a situation where someone I loved received word that a loved one had passed away. I've never really had to console someone for a loss. This was new to me. I was just open with Scott about this, saying, "I don't know what to say. I don't know how to support you."

In the end, just being there and allowing him to feel or process was all I could do.

I did ask Scott, "How could you honour him?" Flying back to attend a funeral looked too expensive, and there was no word on any specific dates. So, instead, Scott had taken the opportunity to "be" with Joe when he went scuba diving the following day. He said it was a great day to scuba dive with Joe and that it was a meaningful day for him.

As I said before, I learned a lot from Scott. I found that I am tapping into my own thoughts and awareness more because I am in a space of respect and openness and honesty, which I have never been in before. I have chosen that in order to be happy, I needed to be who I am. I needed to be me. I learned to see that I still have so much growth in my life, and I have chosen someone (my soulmate) who will support me in that growth.

You may remember that *A Year of Love's* opening page explained what a soulmate is.

> *A **soulmate** isn't someone who completes you. No, a **soulmate** is someone who inspires you to complete yourself. A soulmate is someone who loves you with so much conviction, and so much heart, that it is nearly impossible to doubt just how capable you are of becoming exactly who you have always wanted to be.*
>
> *Bianca Sparacino*

November 2022

Before we had heard about Joe's passing, we were on a boating excursion with about ten other people. It gives me chills to think about this and still inspires me. Scott piped up, just before we were all getting out of the boat, and said, "Thanks, everyone, for making this a great day!"

For me, that was inspiring. I got to watch my man be brave and confident, and he never seemed to wear a *confidence costume* like I so often did. Over the past several months of being in Thailand, I think of the many times I've stepped out of my comfort zone and had to, at least, drape that confidence costume over my shoulder. I think of the time I sparked a conversation with a stranger in a restaurant on Phi Phi Island. Scott was out scuba diving, and I saw this as an opportunity to practice my conversational skills. I got to know this great lady, Paula, and felt confident to share about my book and my Facebook and Instagram profiles. It still dumbfounds me sometimes how I am able to stretch that comfort zone and just be confident.

I know Scott has come from a different world than me. A world of sharing on the spot. A world of saying what he feels. His experiences in AA have contributed to this way of being, I believe. He has said that to me on a few occasions as well, and I find this very inspiring. He is an example and a model of how to be brave, and I use this for my own growth. I still have my own growth in this area, and I pat myself on the back for every step forward.

Scott texted me when he finished "diving with Uncle Joe." He told me it was great to "be with" Uncle Joe. I love that about Scott. He is committed to connecting with people he loves (that's me) and sharing his thoughts and feelings. That is important to me.

Upon Uncle Joe's passing, Scott did something else that totally surprised me. He video called his brother, Ted. Scott has not had a relationship with Ted and often talks about his rough interactions with him growing up. As you may remember from *A Year of Love*, Scott's connections with his family were pretty much non-existent. This news about Joe must have sparked something in Scott that propelled him to connect with his brother.

When Scott called Ted, I did not have any idea who he was. You see, Scott has a lot of old buddies he has been connecting with, and I've met quite a few via video. So, when he was talking to Ted, I thought he must be an old buddy. Although, judging by Scott's interest in communicating with this person, he didn't appear to be a good buddy.

When Scott got off the video call, I asked, "Who was that?"

He told me it was Ted.

I was taken aback to hear it was his brother. I was surprised he didn't introduce me to him. However, I know that just making that video call must have been like being on another planet, and just getting through a conversation about Joe passing was enough to think about.

"I didn't know that was Ted, and I guess I should have asked," I remarked.

"I should have introduced you—sorry," Scott replied.

You see, Scott and I talk a lot about how we are and what is going on in our heads. We know we often forget stuff and don't blame each other for that occurrence. We don't get hung up on the mistakes we make. We just air them out and move on.

I've learned not to take things personally—something I've done so often in the past. When I took things personally, I would build a wall of resentment. I no longer operate this way. Instead, I talk about it calmly and then move on. I think this works well for us and keeps us connected and grounded.

SMCZ: Stretching My Comfort Zone

The author's retreat I just finished got me thinking: *How was I to promote my book and get people excited, especially get them to purchase it?* I decided to start a YouTube channel. What? More to learn and figure out?

I was discovering how capable I really am and learning to do what's needed to reach my destination. Like that sound advice my brother gave me about thirty years ago regarding my worry about the size of my ass—"More cushion for the pushin', Lisa."—I'm reminded of the great advice my new friend John gave us: "Just GTS." I'm sure you figured out what that means—Google That Shit. Thanks, John.

On my YouTube channel*, I shared a quick summary of each chapter in *A Year of Love* without giving too much away. Most importantly, regarding my two-minute blurbs, I was doing something I never thought I could do—talk just off the cuff and make sense. I did it. I really did it! I was proud of myself. I was breaking through the barrier of sharing my thoughts and feelings and expressing myself on the fly.

I learned I was stretching my comfort zone (SMCZ), which was a new awareness. I wasn't stepping out of my comfort zone, because that meant I needed to step back into it. I've realized that my life will have many uncomfortable times, and when I SMCZ, I grow. I

---

* (https://www.youtube.com/channel/UCuM2PhE8lLWV4o1c-xbAkoQ)

expand and land on this new plateau of understanding what I am capable of.

I'm so proud of myself for making big leaps forward. In mid-November I committed myself to finishing my very first book, *A Year of Love*, and getting it to the editor by December. In all my excitement and this newfound passion for writing, I've committed to writing a second book (Yes, this book, *Six Months of Love*) with my author coach, Natasa Denman. But, this time in Thailand was not about spending all my time on my book; it was time to be playful and have some fun.

Scott and I have been travelling around and exploring Thailand together. I appreciate that I get to do all this with Scott. He is open to exploring and seeing the little things and, of course, the big things. We made a quick trip up to Bangkok with our friends and walked around a night market with them. Scott and I were walking hand in hand—and I know things often happen because we send those vibes into the universe—and came across a store with a unique name. It was the Soulmate store—no, it wasn't a shoe store.

"There is our store," I exclaimed.

November 2022

Hey, babe, our "Soulmate Store" in Bangkok

Let me give you some history. When we first met, Scott and I threw around several ways to address each other. My boyfriend, partner, life partner, lover and also soulmate. We loved the depth of what *soulmate* meant. It was like some higher power or the Universe brought us together at that moment, and we were ready to receive each other.

Over the past year and a half, I have understood that I need a partner in my life who truly admires what I do and my passion. A partner who supports my growth and all its ups and downs. A partner who walks outside their personal hell or whatever challenges they have going on and takes the opportunity to really see me. I am blessed that Scott shows me how he can love me. He uses his words and actions daily to express his love, and I share with him what I need from him too.

While in Bangkok, one of the busiest and largest cities I have been to, John, Tiky, Scott and I hopped on a *tuk-tuk*, a three-wheel scooter taxi—a taxi service on steroids, basically (Well, in this crazy city, that's what it felt like). We also took a long boat ride down the Chao Phraya River and experienced Bangkok from a different angle—both the beauty of the temples and, unfortunately, a lot of garbage gathered in the narrow canals. It was on this boat ride that I took a moment to give thanks. Thanks for what I had in my life—a beautiful home, loving family, friends and my health.

Later that day, during an evening walk through a local market, I realized I was getting excited for my kids to join us in Thailand for Christmas. I am so over the moon to have my kids here. I miss them, and I miss seeing them together.

During this past month, I was finalizing the pictures that would go into my first book, and one of them was a picture of me getting tattoos with my kids on Mother's Day. Of course, I needed everyone's approval to have their picture in my book, so when I shared with my kids this particular picture, they were not excited about it. I was disappointed; however, I decided on a brilliant idea: On our walk through a Bangkok market, there was a custom T-shirt designer. He proudly displayed all his T-shirts of happy little kids, married couples and so forth. It was like eureka! I'm going to put that tattoo picture of me and the kids on a T-shirt.

It was an easy process. Pick the size of a white shirt. Send the picture via LINE app, and ten minutes and, I believe, about CAN$12 later—ta da! Crazy, eh? And, of course, when would I wear the shirt? When I pick them up at the airport in December. Oh, I'm so excited!

November 2022

It was great getting to know Tiky and John. They are both such kind, thoughtful people. I love how Tiky shows her big heart by supporting her Thai community. We were all driving together in John and Tiky's truck and were stopped at a red light. A gentleman was selling flowers, which could be hung on the rear-view mirror. Tiky rolls down her window and purchases his beautifully made flower craft. With their custom hand gesture, a slight bow forward and an exchange of *Khob khun kha* (meaning "thank you"), the exchange of love and care was made.

I am blessed to be in the presence of such outward respect and kindness to one's fellow man. Tiky has truly shown me how important family is and how expressing care and attention to others is a priority. Thank you, Tiky.

Phuket

From Bangkok, we took the opportunity to fly to Phuket—and this trip was quite an adventure. From the "holy shit!" of my first scuba dive as a certified open water diver to being part of some of the most emotionally aware moments during these six months of love, this was an incredible trip.

While on our trip, my daughter *Snapchatted* and informed me that her cell phone was getting old and she needed a new one. For me, the immediate feeling was, *OMG, another dishing out of money.* I think I've learned this over my life and has just become the normal way of thinking when a big purchase has to be made. So, I decided I would change the story. I knew I could change the story. I was becoming more aware that I had the power to change the story and how I reacted to it too.

I sat down. I looked at my finances. I looked at how I could support buying my daughter's new phone and who else I can reach out to support in this. I started looking at the prices and phone styles she wanted. This process started to wear on me a little. I was torn between being proud that she knew what she wanted and feeling disappointed that she was asking for what she wanted. I know—it's a little confusing. Yet, I still love that I was able to step back and see that.

Okay, Lisa, deep breath. Just start writing a plan—a proposal to all those involved.

On the plan was—of course—Brianna, her brother, her father and me. With all of us in the plan and acknowledging that this would be her Christmas and birthday present, I could propose a great solution. And I did. I wrote it up and was in consideration of everyone involved and what they could give. Everyone agreed. Not only did all agree, but Brianna would also start paying for her own cell phone bill in the coming year. Yes! A new grown-up responsibility for her, and I was excited for her (and me, too)!

Wow, I was surprised that stepping up to be assertive was paying off. I was feeling more confident in my ideas and following through. I did prepare for any hiccups on this plan. There was one concern about the exact phone she wanted; however, it all worked out. Celebrate the everyday wins, right?

One other learning moment was also communicating with my cell phone company regarding letting my daughter have access to my account, so she could go to a local store in Calgary and purchase the phone. Doing this halfway across the world was another big challenge. Conversations with the cell phone provider happened over Skype, as calling was not on our phone plan and the online service was not working for me. I felt like I dealt with that in my own calm and assertive manner, which Scott listened to as we were in the hotel room one night. I was actually nervous about him hearing my conversation. Nervous that my way wouldn't get what I wanted. I know his way and mine are a lot different due to our personalities and what our parents and upbringing taught us.

In my previous marriage, my former husband did most of that wheeling and dealing when it came to bills and purchases. I trusted my former husband to make great choices, and he always did. As a woman now learning to wade through these new waters, I was now learning to step up and make these choices. I now see and appreciate what my former husband, Stuart, did to make wise decisions with—what seemed like—ease. However, I'm sure he had many moments of stress and uncertainty, like me. I know Scott also learned a way of handling situations, and that's all there is to it. It was my turn now to step up and learn the power that I possessed. I was learning who I was and what I was capable of. I was very proud of my conversations with my cell phone provider.

Another awareness is that I also choose how much energy I put into situations that are not in my control. I know things will work out how they are meant to work out. I know I can do what I can do and be proud that I have put my best foot forward. And that's what I did. After all, Brianna did get the phone, and all those involved in the plan followed through.

* * *

While in Phuket, we visited the Big Buddha with amazing views. As we walked around the towering, 148 ft tall monument, I discerned that Scott was finding a passion for taking pics of the statues everywhere we went. I loved when he shared how he connected with one in particular—the Garuda, a half-man and half-bird creature that bears a large burden. A powerful creature, he has been blessed to achieve anything he wishes. The Thais have been using the Garuda as a royal emblem since the age of the Ayutthaya Empire to symbolize unity.

Scott called me over to see this statue. I read the caption and immediately thought, *This is exactly Scott.*

It's interesting how Scott has two things in common with the Garuda: He is meant for greater things and has a heavy weight on his shoulders. When that weight is lifted, he will truly live and be seen and heard.

When I met Scott, something I saw in him drew me in. I still, to this day, almost have a hard time describing it. It's this greater meaning hidden really deep. It's the message he has inside that deserves to be heard. So, experiencing his *being-ness* at these amazing places has been a blessing.

While at the Big Buddha, I had another moment of pure love with Scott. You see, Scott often does things that totally make my heart flutter and my feelings of love explode. This time it was nothing he did directly to me; it was what he did for his friend. Scott and I were walking around, and I noticed him suddenly talking to someone on his phone. I asked him who it was, and he told me it was a friend he decided to call. I gave him the space to chat and looked around at more statues and read about the Buddha.

When he got off the call, I asked him again about the person he called. He said his friend had never been there before and thought he would video call him and show him around. I loved that he called his friend to include him in the adventure and make his day—an absolutely selfless act of love from my man to another, which inspired me.

November 2022

I told Scott how his gesture to his friend positively impacted me and my day, and it led to purchasing one gold metal heart (a fundraiser for the upkeep of the Buddha) and writing a message on both sides. One side read:

We are all connected. Invite others in to experience life.

The other side of the heart read:

Thank you, Scott, for showing me this today.

Lisa & Scott

That heart is hanging near the Big Buddha in Phuket. If you travel there, look for the heart and take a selfie and share it with me. Also make a choice to impact someone else's life like Scott did that day.

* * *

Riding down the hill on our scooter as we're leaving the Big Buddha, we spotted an elephant sanctuary. What I saw was a tourist spot wherein a smaller elephant, with its leg tied up, was out near the road and a line-up of tourists hoping to get their turn to feed the elephant and rub its trunk. What Scott saw, however, did not sit right with him. He was hit with a tonne of bricks. We did hear that some sanctuaries were more ethical than others. After looking at this for a minute, he shared something quite profound.

"I could feel the sadness in the elephant's eyes," he said.

All I could think of was, *Wow, that level of awareness is so amazing!*

These moments I get to experience with Scott are lessons for me—lessons of being present. Thank you, Scott.

* * *

I love not always having a set plan and taking in the day as it comes. One day we were scootering along, and there was an interesting-looking beach area with what looked like boat rentals. We pulled in and saw we could rent a kayak, so we did. We were unprepared; meaning, we didn't have bathing suits on or anything like that. In the end, did that matter? No. Let's have another experience and have fun!

We rented a kayak, paddled out to a rock island, hung out in our kayak for a while and returned to shore. It's those simple times that are the most abundant.

Phi Phi Island

The next adventure was telling of how well I understood my emotions and what was going on. We took a ferry to Phi Phi Island (Yes, I planned that ferry ride!), and it was the spot where we would scuba dive for the first time together (I'm not considering Mexico last year, as that was part of my lessons for certification). This was our first scuba excursion wherein I would be Scott's dive partner, and he mine.

When we arrived on the island, we carried four bags to our hotel under a scorching thirty-degree heat. To top it off, we still needed to find a scooter rental place and dive shops to organize our scuba trips. I was feeling heavy and low.

"Are you okay?" Scott asked as we were walking down the street.

I broke down.

I wasn't sure what exactly was going on; however, I shared that I was feeling stressed. Stressed about scuba diving for the first time. Stressed about the feeling of holding Scott back. Stressed about the

November 2022

fact that I was going 60 ft underwater with sea life and that it was up to me to breathe slowly and be certain about my actions, the skills I'd learned and trust in the people I was diving with.

Scott brought me in close and reassured me that he had heard me. He said he felt something was up with me, that our different levels of experience were not an issue to him, and it was really just about exploring the ocean and seeing its wonders. He reaffirmed me that I would be okay and that I would do great.

Scott always seemed to know exactly what to say. I was proud that I spoke up and got it out of my system. Don't get me wrong; I was still nervous and scared. However, I knew that this fear was something I could push through. I knew I had this in me. It's taken time to understand this about myself; however, I know it's there, always stretching my comfort zone.

After the four dives together in Phi Phi, I learned a few things: I can do anything when I know fear is holding me back. I can experience anything once, and then decide if this is a passion I would love to do more of. I also learned that it is important to be heard. To talk. To share. To trust in my partner. I also deserve Scott—a partner who is open and supportive to hear me and my challenges. This is what I've always wanted in my life. I deserve someone who hears me and provides a space for me to share yet doesn't solve my problems and never dismisses them. He respects the space when I share, and I definitely deserve that.

Phi Phi was an adventure, for sure. We had just gone on a really amazing walk up to a lookout area and were wowed by the view. However, the next day, my view was the inside of a toilet. I caught something—probably from the eggplant bake I had at a restaurant the night before. Oh, I thought I was dying! Coming out both ends and bedridden for twenty-four hours. Ohhhh, not fun at all. Scott, on the other hand, planned his own day of scuba diving. Of course, he took care of me with water, salad and enough snacks to eat and get something in my tummy. I had enough diving for now.

How many steps?

Next, we went to Krabi, a beautiful resort town. We took a bus to a more remote location to kayak along a peaceful river, where trees and rocks just seemed to pop out of nowhere. It was a beautiful float through the water, and I appreciated the beauty of it all. Scott knows I love spending this serene time with him—time I've discovered is so important. Time we both truly cherish together.

In Krabi we found our next great memory—the Tiger Cave Temple. We walked into the temple area, not knowing what was ahead of us. What would we see? What would we discover? We started our walk over to the bottom of the tiger area, not knowing if they were statues of tigers or real tigers. What was this all about? We often take on adventures without focussing too much on the historical background of the spot we visit, and instead enjoy the surprise brought by the space and adventure.

We arrived at a daunting flight of stairs, built from stone. We started on our way up, not knowing what was ahead. The stairs were often fairly narrow and had a long string between them. We started the trek, then read the sign: 1,260 steps to the top. Little did either of us really know what that would look like. We knew, though, that we would make it up there, come hell or high water.

There was one advantage going for us. The walk was mostly in the shade. Thank goodness! Our hearts were pumping hard, and we each had a bottle of water for the frequent stops. People coming down reassured us that the climb was worth it.

It was late afternoon, and the grind of the climb was soon behind us. When we arrived at the top, the view was breathtaking! Monks were cleaning the spacious temple grounds, as people walked around in awe of the magnificent view of the mountainous jungle below. It was within an hour before the sun was setting, and like many others, we thought to stay up to see the sun set; it was the perfect spot for such a thing! However, in the distance looked like a nasty rain cloud. As cool as it would be to see the sunset, I would not be excited to walk down slippery, wet and narrow rock steps.

I was right. You know, listen to your gut. As we were about one-fourth down the stairs, the rain started. I had flip-flops on, and they needed to come off, as my feet were slipping in them. Barefoot, thank goodness, worked out okay.

What an accomplishment—1,260 steps up and 1,260 steps down! Another great feat for the dynamic duo of Lisa and Scott.

Cat's balls

My relationship with Brianna seemed to be expanding and improving. We have more chats on Snapchat, yet I feel like I still have so much more to improve upon in this relationship.

One day, she sent me a picture of cat testicles on Snapchat. When she sent that picture, I wasn't quite sure what I was looking at, and at the same time, I knew exactly what I was looking at—pinky, bloody balls laying on what looked like some surgical paper.

You see, Brianna was taking a course called Veterinary Technical Assistant Certificate. She decided to live on campus at Olds College, Alberta for the four month-duration of the course. I was very proud of her for doing this. Of course, money was needed for gas and some extra food, and she did not work while taking those studies, as her work was an hour away back in Calgary.

"Is that what I think they are?" I replied to her Snap.

Yes, she was part of the removal of a cat's testicles and, of course, quickly snapped a shot to send to her mommy. Oh, thank you, my daughter. Ewwww!

But more importantly, I was grateful that Brianna was interacting with me and reaching out to me. I was truly grateful for this.

November 2022

GRATITUDE THOUGHT: I AM VERY AWARE THAT I BELIEVED THE MANY STORIES TOLD TO ME, AND I RECONFIRMED THOSE BELIEFS OVER AND OVER IN MY LIFE. I AM GRATEFUL THAT I HAVE THIS AWARENESS ABOUT SCOTT TOO. THE STORIES HE WAS TOLD ABOUT HIM HAS BEEN RECONFIRMED OVER AND OVER AGAIN. I AM GRATEFUL THAT I CAN BE WITH HIM ON HIS JOURNEY OF THIS AWARENESS.

CHAPTER 5

December 2022

I AM EXCITED, SAD, PROUD, CONNECTED, INSPIRED, ADVENTUROUS

Christmas, for me, holds great memories—laughter, family time, singing, delicious food and giving presents. I looked forward to doing most of those things on a different level here in Thailand with my kids.

I realized, over this year, the significance of the memories and experiences we share with people, like when I got tattoos with my kids or a nose piercing with my best friend, Sandra. Shared memories and feeling the love and care that goes along with spending time with the most important people in your life matter most. So, Christmas was about adventure, exploring and time together, not about the presents—although I couldn't resist making a stocking full of goodies for when the kids woke up Christmas morning.

I decided that a plant in our rental house would be the Christmas tree and decorated this with silver balls and wrapped the pot in a wrap-around skirt that I had bought to cover my arms during a temple visit. I was ready for the kids and to make new memories.

Oh, I do love Christmas, and I wanted to do something special for my kids. This was Scott and my first Christmas as a married couple too. I considered ordering a big turkey or ham dinner from a local business and having a yummy feast. I also booked a fun event for us on Christmas day to learn how to cook a few local Thai dishes. It included visiting a Thai market, buying local produce and going back and making the dishes. Also, we needed to see elephants, temples and caves and get a Thai massage, along with other fun events planned for when they came. I was excited for this.

Scott knows how important my kids are to me. That is one thing we learned a few days after we first met when we attended a relationship course together. The presenter, Mr. Tim O'Kelly, pointed out that the children always come first for women and, technically, the man or partner is further down her list. This was an eye-opener for Scott (and me too). I knew that my kids were a priority, my blood, my flesh. I would do anything for them.

One night when we were hanging out, he said, "I look forward to spending time with the kids when they come."

The times when Scott declares things like this really send it home for me. His understanding of what is important and how he simply shares those feelings are what I truly love about this man. He has a very big heart.

December 2022

House update

After living in our house for over a month now, we were almost used to the howling dogs at night and soon discovered we had some new house friends—geckos that climbed the stucco walls outside, and we often found them inside too. They were harmless and probably were more scared of us; they often quickly ran away when discovered. Although, at this point, we spotted something a little uglier. We had some cockroaches around the house, mostly around the wet bathroom drains, and we sometimes caught them scurrying around cupboards in the kitchen, which, to me, meant something was dirty. Although I came to understand that that was probably not the case, as when I mostly found them, they were in the pull-out drawers that only had a few pots inside.

Besides the geckos and cockroaches, I was taken aback one day when Scott and I were cooking in the kitchen. I looked above the shelf where he was cooking and saw a black, rather hefty-sized rodent run across the shelf and back behind the spices! It threw me for a quick jump up on the bench nearby. I was totally disgusted by the fact that there was a rat in our house and, even more gross, in our kitchen.

We informed our wonderful landlord, Noi, and she promptly got us some rat traps. Over the next few weeks, we captured a few rats on a sticky pad and disposed of them in the garbage outside. Everything went into the garbage. Noi figured out that the stove vent was pushed forward, and that's where they appeared to be coming in. After pushing it back, the problem was solved. Yes!

Six Months Of Love

Pride in me

It was December 1st, and I achieved 40,824 words for my book, *A Year of Love*. Yes! I needed to reach at least 25,000 and no more than 40,000—the package offered through the Ultimate 48 Hour Author was for a 40,000-word book. Thankfully, Natasa did offer some leeway on those 824 words over my limit. I was super excited about completing this big goal and getting my book to the editor. I was proud of the work I put in. I was proud of the new things I was doing.

Speaking of new things, we were planning to attend a personal development course in Phoenix in September, which required booking a hotel. When I did my homework and figured out prices, it was much more than we anticipated, so I took it upon myself to find other accommodations. The price difference between the hotel close by and the hotel venue was over CAN$1,000. That's quite the difference. That's a lot of money for gas in the '69 Dodge Dart we planned to drive down there.

After doing my price searching, I confidently told Scott what I found out and thought we should book the nearer hotel since we would have our own transportation and, really, it was only five minutes away.

"I trust your decisions," Scott said to me. It's that sort of respect I get from Scott.

I'm also learning to trust myself in making decisions. I've learned that I'm smart enough and human, that even with all my research, I can still make a bad choice and be good with that. Through the work I've done and the support from Scott, I've learned that not only do I trust myself in making choices but I can also learn from my mistakes.

December 2022

Connection

Scott and I were returning home from a day of exploring and visiting some caves. As we were admiring the scenery while riding along, we happened to look at a house and both thought it looked like a church. Its type of windows made it so.

The connection between our thoughts is interesting. It's like Scott and I are attuned to spotting things; when one of us says something, the other is thinking the same. It's neat how we have these similar insights into things and verbalize them too. For sure, it's a comforting feeling to have someone meet you at the same level.

We talk a lot about our feelings, and this connects us. We openly share and feel heard. Don't get me wrong, we are not perfect at this; however, we stay open to sharing and knowing that we will allow for the space without judgement. No criticism. Only understanding, support and knowledge that we can do this because we trust, love and care for each other.

An emotional drain

Scott sits across the table from me on his computer as I sit on mine, our asses sweating—something I was definitely not used to close to Christmas time. I'm from Canada, where it snows from November to April. We just finished our egg scramble, which Scott made.

My first book, *A Year of Love*, has been sent to my editor. I was looking forward to seeing what changes and corrections needed to be made. This is another learning curve of mine. I was excited to see where I could improve. Understanding that I am always learning in this life, I now look at challenges or "failures" more as opportunities. How can I learn from them? What can I learn? I find this very exciting.

One important detail about being an author and publishing a book was that my name was about to be put in stone. So, in a quick discussion with my author coach, I decided to print my book as Lisa Brearley, even though I haven't legally changed my name yet.

Making that change was important to me. I knew I wanted to write more books (like this one) and also did not want to confuse my readers. More importantly, I was honoured to take Scott's last name. I am so proud of him taking on this new role as an author, as he sits across from me typing out his first book.

I know the book he is writing is a real emotional drain on him. I see it in how his fingers peck the individual keys and get the words out. Reliving the trauma and emotional turmoil that was his life must surely be hard. It is, again, very inspiring to see. I've watched him expand his ability to trust and use computers so much since I met him. Does he have days of total disgust and hatred towards technology? You bet.

That reminds me of looking at challenges as opportunities to grow. I told Scott I would get his website going—a new learning opportunity for me! So, I've been learning a lot of new lingo and how to do this. I've recently got it up and running with links to pay and set up appointments. Crazy from someone who used to say, "Can you fix this computer problem?" to someone who knew more. I'm learning how to GTS—Google That Shit—and find out answers for myself. (Thanks, John!)

I'm still learning how to get Scott's website easily googled on the World Wide Web. I think my next step is to ask the peeps I know.

December 2022

That's another learning of mine—reach out for support. Someone else will know or at least help point you in the right direction.

It's interesting that anything can happen when you stay open to possibilities. I've been wondering if I really want to go back to teaching full time. I'm not very interested in going back to the grind of working a full day and the planning, assessment and meetings that need to happen. Don't get me wrong, I absolutely loved going to work every day and teaching kids. It was like it wasn't work (except for when it came to report cards, and then it was work).

I enjoyed every minute of it—teaching kids and seeing their eyes light up when they got something for the first time or even seeing them struggle. I loved their inquisitive nature, and I loved being the person that they enjoyed seeing every day. It gave me great pride to have parents talk about how their child loves coming to school and would love to have me as their teacher the following year.

I knew the positive start I had with my mom as my kindergarten teacher stayed with me over the years, and I was kind of honouring Mom and all the work she has done with kids over the years. Being a teacher was what I've wanted to be all my life. There was only one bump in the road along the way where I thought teaching was not going to happen for me.

You see, when I was young, I would invite neighbours over to play school. I remember the round table downstairs with the tall shelf full of books beside it. I would teach the neighbours and give them tests. I had always felt like this was where I wanted to be.

As I grew up, and it was time to go to university, I applied to enter the Bachelor of Education program at the University of Prince Edward Island—nothing else and nowhere else. It was just meant to be; this was where I was going and what I was doing.

It didn't quite happen that way.

Like most who apply to programs at university, I would find out via a letter in the mail if I got in or not. The day came when I received my letter, and it read:

Our sincerest apologies ... you were not accepted into the BEd program. ... You will be put on a waiting list. You are first on the list.

What? Not in? How could this be? My dreams were pretty much shattered that day. After several months of sweating over whether one person would pull out of the program and I would be in was finally over. Thank goodness—I was accepted!

After graduating from UPEI in 1995, I did a short stint as a teacher's assistant in P.E.I., then married and moved across the country to Calgary, Alberta. I immediately enquired with the Calgary Board of Education (CBE), the public teaching system, but had no luck. It took a few years to get in with the board after volunteering with Mrs. Talerico in her Grade 2 class. Thanks to her, I got to know how a public Calgary school operates and looks like. I enjoyed being in her class.

I've appreciated the different teaching contracts over the years with CBE. Fortunately, I was not working full time when my two amazing children were born, and I only chose to work full time for about the last ten years of my career.

This year, I took a leave of absence and have looked at my life differently. I'm learning more about myself and how I can make different choices and stand up for myself. I'm learning that I am capable of living a life I want to create. The question is ... what do I want to create?

December 2022

With time on my hands and enough downtime, I've carefully looked at this question a lot since coming to Thailand. I kept reminding myself that I do have a lot to offer. I really did have to remind myself because I continued to doubt that I was capable enough to make such big changes in my life.

I've done a lot of changes so far and have made some *crazy* decisions compared to what the *old Lisa* may have done. Remember when I said that when you are open to new possibilities, new things can happen to you? Well, I asked Scott if he wanted to take a walk to the local coffee shop we had visited before. It's a neat little spot; quiet and overlooks a pond. The coffee and sweet treats were delicious. Upon returning to our house from the coffee shop, we ran into an older gentleman named Ted Guhl. He stopped on his scooter, asking if we lived at the place we were renting. We chatted and found out that Ted was an artist, rented a house close by and was looking to rent a new place, as his was being sold.

As we chatted more, he learned that I was a teacher and was open to the possibility that I could teach while I was here in Thailand. He began to tell us that a school was right up the street from our rental. He said it was called HALIO (Hua Hin Learning International Organization). He gave me his business card, and we said our goodbyes. I knew this wasn't just a coincidence. I knew things were put in front of me at the right time.

Upon looking up HALIO online, I fell in love with their philosophy and what they stood for. I sent my resume to the email on Ted's card and anxiously waited for his reply. Ted had texted the owners, Padma and John, regarding my interest. They replied with what I needed to send to a specific email for the school and that there was a good possibility they were hiring for a kindergarten teacher.

It took me a few days to kind of catch my breath again. Is this an opportunity for me to positively impact these young minds and put my experience and personal development I have found so influential in my life to great use? Is this my calling? Is this what the Universe is saying to me?

As with any positive endeavour one takes, they need to prepare if it doesn't work out as well. If I get an interview and don't get the job, I will appreciate the experience of going for an interview, as it has been decades since I had one.

However I look at it, meeting Ted that day confirmed that using my positive mindset and seeing life as full of opportunities was working for me. I need to remain open to new experiences and take the challenges as they come.

A great experience

Scott and I needed to book a trip out of Thailand to get our passports stamped to extend our stay (something I admit I didn't totally understand, as I knew we were under a six-month travel visa; however, it got us exploring some more). So, we planned a trip to Da Nang, Vietnam. We didn't do too much research on this place at this time of year, and when we arrived, the weather was fairly cool and wet.

The night we arrived, it was dark and late, and we were hungry. We walked up the street where our hotel was, looking for a place to eat. We saw little animals running across and realized—*Eeeewwww!* They were rats.

We have said that visiting Da Nang, Vietnam was a good trip, although we had moments when we were turned off and it was

December 2022

challenging to have fun. Don't get me wrong, I was grateful for the adventure and the fact that we got plane tickets and accommodations for about CAN$800, had a cute hotel to stay in and had each other. However, the weather sucked (mostly rainy and cold—well, by the standards we just came from), the food was mostly not conducive to what we needed to eat (for Scott's diabetes and my routine of lots of veggies), and our stomachs turned almost every day.

As I sat in our hotel lobby, I was very grateful to have met a Canadian couple also staying at our hotel. They were about to head out the next day to see Marble Mountain and the Lady Buddha. They asked if we would like to join them in the cab and share the cost. I appreciated the ask and gladly accepted.

This giving and receiving thing has come up in my life on many occasions. I'm learning to hear that others are offering to help, support or have you join them not out of pity but because they like you or are interested in you or maybe you're just a fun person to hang out with. So, we joined them on this full-day adventure, and the sun shone that day in more ways than one. We got to hang out with some cool Canadian people, including the friendly cab driver. We got to see Marble Mountain and the Lady Buddha. And we spent time together.

I believe the Lady Buddha was also a highlight for Scott, as his fascination with taking pictures of statues became his "thing." He would often post them on his social media, and I could tell he admired the work and how stoic they were. He later posted those statue pictures with quotes of the day on social media to promote his online coaching business, Forward Walking Choices Coaching. I love his connection to cool stuff like this and how he makes those connections on a more spiritual level.

* * *

Thanks to meeting Ted Guhl, I had an interview over Zoom with the owner of HALIO while we were in Vietnam. Padma and I spoke for over an hour regarding the position, what HALIO was like and what my desires were in Thailand. I knew what I knew, and that was teaching in the kindergarten and Grade ½ level. So when I approached the kindergarten teacher position at HALIO, it was based on what I previously knew. Padma informed me of the many differences, such as the reduced pay, the level of qualifications and expectations required for that position, and the fact that I would be entering as an experienced teacher when it was more appropriate for a beginner teacher.

We ended the interview with the understanding that the position was not for me; however, I regarded our interview as a great experience while meeting someone new. It was a great opportunity. I hadn't had an interview in over fifteen years. Later on, I'd connect with Mr. Vince, the principal, and start volunteering once per week in the new year. I was really excited for this opportunity.

The stopover, the stayover, the return

We were on our last day in Da Nang, heading back to Bangkok. I was getting excited, as I knew that when we returned, we would pick up the kids! I was ready to wear the shirt with the large photo of us getting tattoos together when we met them at the airport.

Since Calgary's time zone was behind us by fourteen hours, the kids had made their way to the airport. They informed me, via Snapchat, that the plane was a little behind. Their itinerary was a layover in Vancouver, then a stop in Tokyo before landing in Bangkok. Simple, right?

December 2022

Well, that wasn't how it all played out. It wasn't simple.

After confirming that they were getting on their Calgary flight to Vancouver, I breathed a sigh of relief. They were on their way. They arrived in Vancouver, and I got a Snapchat from my daughter, explaining that the plane was too late to make their connecting flight to Tokyo.

I called my kids to see what they were doing to remedy the situation. Another flight out? A different route? Maybe a hotel room, at least? Well, the airline did not seem to be helpful. Not only were they *not* told in Calgary that their delayed flight would not connect on time with the flight leaving Vancouver, but their next available flight out to possibly come to Thailand would be five days later. To top it off, there were no available flights back to Calgary for three days!

I felt so many feelings—sad, angry, disappointed, broke. At that same time, all I could think was, *Ohhh, my poor babies.*

However, they were not babies. They manned up and stood in line for eight hours to get the answers about the five-day or three-day wait. I guess I had to man up too. It was an expense I didn't think about. I had to send money for food and for transportations so they could get around. Their father kindly got them a hotel room for the three-day stay in Vancouver. Thank goodness for that! I'm very appreciative.

I'm grateful they had each other, but at the same time, I was so heartbroken and saddened that this Christmas trip to Thailand was ruined. I was so heartbroken.

I called them on Christmas day, as they were still in Vancouver, and I was filled with tears and sadness. I spoke to them and did my best to express my feelings of love and that I missed them. You know, expressing myself with my kids is still a growth area for me. I struggled not knowing if I was getting my feelings out there.

The kids arrived back home in Calgary to an empty house, as their father was away for Christmas. It saddened me. However, I chose to look at it as them being safe and having each other. Now it was time to see about rebooking those flights. Oh my goodness, don't get me started on that.

Christmas day for us was more or less uneventful. We didn't exchange Christmas presents, no big dinner and no kids to celebrate the holidays with us. This feeling of loss was probably one of the reasons for the continued intestinal annoyance from our travels to Vietnam.

On December 28, we decided to get out of the house. We were mostly done with the traveller's diarrhea (the lovely gift we got in Vietnam) and just needed to get out. With a few days left in 2022, we took the scooter out for an hour ride out of Hua Hin. We ate at this great restaurant on the water, stopped at another temple and saw another cave we could explore. We had no idea what this cave was all about. All we saw was a sign, and we were usually up for seeing something cool.

We rode down the clay road for a few kilometres and saw the entrance where we had to pay CAN$8 for both of us to get in. Of course, it was significantly cheaper for locals to get in, and it should be. There were no other cars or scooters parked in the parking lot. Just as we parked our bike and paid the fee, the lady picked up a bag, pulled out a flashlight, and asked in her best English, "Do you need a flashlight?"

We didn't exactly know why she offered flashlights, so we just signalled and mumbled that we had phones with lights (and we also knew we had lots of battery power).

December 2022

We started up the side of the mountain, watching for directional arrows to guide our way. The steps were haphazardly placed rocks, and there was cement scraping into them to increase traction as you stepped up. We've climbed similar areas, and we knew we could handle it. A few minutes up, and there was the entrance to the cave. I looked down into the big hole and saw that it did look dark in there and now had an idea why the lady had suggested the flashlights. Well, little did we know exactly what we were getting into.

We made our way down the stairs into the opening of the cave. The terrain was rocky and not always clear. It was cool to see large pieces of rock, which I believe may be identified as stalagmites and stalactites, all over the place.

Because we used our phones to light the way, taking pictures wasn't always easy. We continued on our way, and if we didn't take notice of where we were walking or if water had dripped down from the ceiling, we might have ended up in a situation that could be really bad. You see, there were major drop-offs and large open holes. This could have been a really bad situation for someone with poor balance or poor shoes.

We were five to ten minutes in, taking our time and seeing if we could get a possible picture or two. About fifteen minutes in, I started to feel unsure of the space I was in. This was a state I have not experienced very often. I started visualizing problems that could happen—a large rock falling, an earthquake, slipping, falling. I could feel myself getting hotter. I could feel my heartbeat racing faster. It felt like I was beginning to have a panic attack.

I know from the work I've done over the past several years that these are all thoughts I can manage. It took some time to allow my body to know this. Also, it helped that Scott encouraged and reminded me that I was capable of doing this.

I knew I had to do a few things. I knew I needed to ask Scott to be patient. I knew I needed to let him know how I was feeling. So, I expressed my feelings of worry, fright and uncertainty. I also had to start breathing (Even as I write this, my heartbeat is picking up). Breathing was one tool I'd learned over the past few years that grounded me, so I took deep breaths and blew them out with some sound. Next—and I learned this from my experience over the years of going to the dentist, which I hate—is to visualize myself at the end. I saw myself going out of the cave and seeing the light at the end.

As I practiced all this stuff, I thought I needed to prove that even if the lights were off, I would still be okay. So, I asked Scott to shut his light off, and I would too. It was as pitch dark as dark could be. I took the time to breathe in that dark space (knowing I had a good footing on the ground).

When we put our lights back on, I was still quite hesitant, even though I was going through all these calming motions. Scott reminded me that if we needed to use the additional battery to keep a phone lit, it would mean that we would only have one phone lighting our way. So, with that, we proceeded to keep going and following the arrows that were often difficult to see.

About twenty-five minutes in, Scott saw some light, and I began to breathe a sigh of relief. We got closer to it; however, the path led us in the opposite direction. Again, a little panic set in.

Breathe, Lisa. Visualize the end, Lisa. You can do this, Lisa.

With Scott's clear and direct understanding that we can get through this and my certainty that I am in control of how I feel, we arrived at the end. A park attendant was stationed at the exit. Though he hadn't spoken to us, I believe he was there to save anyone who needed support on their journey through the cave.

As we walked out onto the fresh air with the bright sky, I took the time to appreciate that I made it. I made it!

Mmmmm, chocolate

I ended the last day of 2022 with a visit to The Chocolate Factory. Scott had gone for a Thai massage, and I walked down the street to the yummiest place on earth—The Chocolate Factory.

I sat in the restaurant section after eyeing the package of dark chocolate I wanted to buy after I had enjoyed my coffee. And that I did. I bought the yummy dark chocolate pieces and sat outside while eating them. They were really good, and I enjoyed most of them and saved the rest for later.

As a kid, the "cheap" chocolate was my treat of choice. Today, I've matured, and dark chocolate is what I choose, and it's better for me; I get the satisfaction of chocolate in my mouth and also don't overeat it. It was a lovely late afternoon venture for me.

In the evening, Scott and I headed out for an early dinner at LaMer restaurant—where we had eaten several times before. We quite loved their shrimp cakes. After our shrimp cake fill, we headed to Starbucks to get some caffeine in us, so we could actually make it to midnight to see in the New Year.

After caffeinating and video chatting with Sandra, we were off to the beach to meet Terry and Nam and watch the fireworks. It was great to have friends to celebrate such occasions together. Unfortunately, our paths never crossed that night, and somehow we could not figure out where each other was along the beach. All good, though. Scott and I enjoyed each other's company, walking hand in hand up the beach. Fireworks were going off in the distance throughout the evening before the midnight countdown happened.

Of course, when you're tired, you sometimes make not-so-great choices. We were both thinking this; however, Scott said it out loud. "Let's stop at the night market and get a treat."

So, that's what we did. This amazing woman who makes homemade *donairs* and roti has been a reminder to us of the beautiful people in this world. We stopped at her little food station to see her once again. Every time we stroll by her station or stop for a snack, she is so welcoming with her big smile and, of course, great food. We always watch her in admiration of her skill in creating such delicious food. Yes, we both had a roti treat that night—Nutella on top for me. Happy New Year to us!

We headed back home and rang in the new year in bed, barely awake, with a good night and a kiss, exclaiming we stayed up.

December 2022

GRATITUDE THOUGHT: SCOTT ATTENDS ONLINE SUPPORT SESSIONS, AND WHEN OTHERS SHARE ABOUT THEIR SUCCESSES IN THEIR LIFE JOURNEY, HE SHOWS THEM. I OVERHEARD HIM ON A FEW OCCASIONS YELLING, "YAHOO!" I ABSOLUTELY LOVE THIS IN MY MAN—BEING COMFORTABLE TO EXPRESS HIMSELF AND BEING A POSITIVE SUPPORT FOR OTHERS.

CHAPTER 6

January 2023

I AM WORRIED, INVIGORATED, STRONG, PISSED OFF, STEPPING UP

Now that 2023 has arrived, it was time to make some goals. Scott and I both made a vision board. A board where we saw where we wanted to be by the end of the year. We printed these vision board posters in colour and posted them proudly on the wall in the kitchen of our rental. We were excited for bigger and better things for ourselves and knew we were highly capable.

Did we have doubts that it would all come to us? Of course. Were we delusional? No. We were smart when we came to Thailand, not knowing if I was getting a teaching job or not here. We planned finances the best we could and still have backup from three property rentals back home in Canada.

On my vision board, I said I would have two books published by December 31, 2023—*A Year of Love* and *Six Months in Thailand*. I would work on co-authoring a book with my mom about my memory of making pie with her as a young child in the restaurant we owned, where she made the absolute best pies (and still does to this day). Scott was getting his online coaching business going, making a comfortable income and setting his own hours. We were also geared up to start a year-long coaching course through the personal development company where we met. It was an online course where we could see our vision board come to fruition and expand our comfort zone.

Back in class

On January 5th, I had my first day volunteering at HALIO. I was excited and nervous. I met the kindergarten kids and worked with a small group of seven kids ready to move on to the next level. I brought in some sea glass and did a little Five Senses lesson with them. They loved it. I loved it. I also worked with another student over the lunch hour; we took the time to get to know each other, and he shared his work on his iPad. I appreciated this opportunity and felt a little nostalgic about my teaching days, wondering if I was supposed to get back to teaching, as this was a passion of mine and I knew I was good at it.

I enjoyed my first day of volunteering and was glad that I could give back in this manner and share my skills and passion for children to see the best in themselves. I set several hours every Monday for volunteering. I planned mini lessons with the small group and supported another student with his studies over the lunch hour.

The following week I read a book about a giraffe who needed glasses to see better. The kids enjoyed predicting what was coming

January 2023

next in the story. I pulled out my art book and showed them how it took me several attempts to draw the giraffe I liked. We all drew the giraffe together and learned about what really makes a giraffe (all those details). It was a fun lesson.

Food and Botox

At this point, we know our new friends, John and Tiky, fairly well. I was feeling grateful, as Tiky had invited me out with some of her friends and we travelled together to a local restaurant about half an hour from Hua Hin. It was the coolest experience. I got to experience cooking with the ladies in Thai style. They all chipped in; I asked to help, and they just wanted me to watch.

Nam deboned fish for the meal. Tiky cut and cooked up some veggies and made a homemade sauce for the dish she was making. They ordered some extra food like snails, and the other ladies cooked too. It was an interesting experience. I did my best to contribute to the conversation, which varied from food to Botox.

I saw more love in my life by being open and accepting those who invited me to be with them. It's a sign of love and care. I was starting to see more that I was worth all that I had. I deserved the love. I deserved the care. I deserved it.

PLD all over again

The year-long online coaching course that Scott and I joined was a brand-new program for the personal development company. We paid big money for this course, and it was a rough start getting the time zone difference worked out and communicating through the online platform. It was a challenge, for sure. It felt like our Pacesetters Leadership Dynamics (PLD) experience, which I extensively talked about in *A Year of Love*, was happening all over again.

At this point, though, Scott and I both were in a refined place of growth and awareness. Scott worked well on routine, like many of us. However, when you have learning challenges and so many life experiences around lack of trust, like Scott does, it can compound and feel like support is utterly non-existent. Scott felt like he was not being heard and supported, like in PLD. He had some great conversations with one lady working for the business, who supported him, got him through many of the tough days and listened to his concerns with the admin of this program.

I, on the other hand, found it much easier to deal with challenges when they arose. I was in no way in competition with Scott on how we dealt with these things; however, it was worth noticing as we were on our respective journeys.

Scott and I have been through all the courses offered by the personal development business we had met at, and now they were stepping it up for this brand new year-long course. It had never been done before, and they were calling us the pioneers. This year-long course was not only an investment financially; it was an investment in time too. Both are worthy of me and my growth.

I had nerves, fear and some anxiety running through me with this course. The biggest was just speaking and sharing my feelings in front of the group. During a group meeting of 100 participants, I put up my virtual hand and shared my thoughts about not knowing my end goal and that I was sort of lost and unclear about what I wanted to achieve.

January 2023

What stuck with me the most about sharing was what came next.

"So, how's that working for you?" asked the presenter in an authoritative tone. Like my experience back at the week-long course where I had met Scott in 2021, I felt stupid. I felt lost in my answer. I didn't feel present. I felt like my mind was blank. Seeing this in myself has been so hard to overcome.

"Well, Lisa," the presenter proceeded to say, "pretend you are the coach, and you are coaching me. What would you say to me?"

I froze and said something like, "Oh, well then, what is your passion or inspiration? What are you good at?"

I then went blank. I had a hard time thinking on the spot about what to say, confirming that my thoughts and ideas didn't matter and that I could not eloquently share them with others. My confidence in this area comes in waves. I have good days, and other days I lack the ability to show up for myself and others and just share. I'm learning and I'm aware of it—which is one of the biggest challenges—and I am open to moving forward with this. It's a beautiful and scary thing, and I embrace it all.

Besides really looking at myself and who I was showing up as, I was starting to have some more insight into how I showed up for others, especially my husband. I am learning to step outside of myself and see how to share him with the world because I truly believe he is a special person. A person who needs to be seen and heard.

I was excited for the coaching course I was on with Scott. We were making big goals and were highly dedicated. Scott was bound and determined to get his online coaching off, and I was determined to write and publish my books. My goal was to share my book in front of ten live audiences. That was big for me. Could I really do this? In my heart, I knew I could; however, I was freaking out about the idea.

I've seen so much growth in myself over the past few years that I knew I would get there eventually and needed to be gentle with myself. I knew it would come. Not sure when. Not sure where. Not sure how much. I just knew it would come. How did I know? I'm putting in the work. I'm putting in the dedication. I'm opening up to opportunities. I'm listening to my gut. I'm loving my life.

By January 5, I was recording the explanation of the last chapter of *A Year of Love* for my YouTube channel. Wow, what an accomplishment! I was proud that I had recorded fourteen videos with no script and just a few words to remind myself of what I wanted to cover. I knew these videos were a great experience for me. They support me in working up to speak in front of ten live audiences.

The first live audience I chose to speak in front of was my family. We Skype every other Sunday, so I prepped them with an email, saying I wanted to share my book with them on our next call.

My most vocal fan, my mom, got back to me with overwhelming love and support. My dad had not responded; however, he did make it that night. My three other siblings didn't respond at all and ended up not coming due to other appointments. I chose not to dwell on why they did not really come. There was a part of me that questioned that, for sure. Did they really not care about what I needed? Was I not clear about that? What were they really thinking about my choice to write a book and how I'm choosing to live my life with more purpose and meaning?

January 2023

My first "live" book share with my parents

My thoughts of self-doubt and unworthiness did swirl around a lot in my head. However, I knew it was up to me how I reacted to them not replying to the email or their absence from the Skype call. All I knew was that this was a sharing and speaking opportunity for me, no matter who showed up. And, yes, Mom and Dad were there and supported me in listening to what my book was about, and they shared that they were both very proud of me.

I learned from that Skype call that not everyone (even your family) is ready to hear you. And that's okay. I chose to remain grounded, knowing what I am doing feels right and makes me happy.

Writing and sharing my positive mindset in life makes me happy. Going through challenges and finding ways to expand my comfort zone is what makes me happy. I am happy.

Six Months Of Love

Small important things

Sometimes it's the small things that add up to make the big things, and appreciating that is what makes life so great. We were out one evening at a local Thai market, and Scott was excited when he got a fabulous deal on some Harley shirts. This market is only open on Tuesday nights and is a crazy, busy spot where vendors come from all around Thailand to show their wares.

Scott came home and strutted his stuff, showing off his new shirts. It was a great time to take pictures of Scott posing in his new shirts and bragging all about it. He really is a handsome man, and I love sharing this with the world and letting them know how much I care for him. Letting him know how much I care for him is what is really, truly important.

Friends are also important, too, and I am slowly learning how to share and be present with friends, both old and new. We had the opportunity to celebrate John's birthday, and his wife Tiky asked us to be part of the surprise event. We were so honoured and blessed to be a part of this.

Our group of thirteen enjoyed conversation and great food at an amazing restaurant. These are moments I am truly blessed to be a part of, and I do my best to step forward to let others know how much I appreciate them, which I do through communicating and connecting with them. This has been lacking for me for many years. I've just been okay with being in my own space, and I'm now starting to see that being with others is so fulfilling and makes life much richer.

For the birthday dinner, we all dressed up (all in a white theme, a cool idea from Tiky), and I was lookin' good; I thought I could take some selfies. I don't usually do this comfortably. I've found taking selfies

January 2023

a little self-centred and snobbish, but I slowly learned to appreciate it. It's about self-love and being proud of myself. It's about sharing myself with the world, recognizing how beautiful I am, both inside and out, and feeling great about that. I sure have had some interesting shifts in my life, and showing myself off to the world has been one of them. I am worthy of sharing. I am worth it.

As I said before, keeping a connection with friends is so extremely important. A few days later, we had a beautiful evening with some of the Thailand crew (Tiky, John, Terry and Nam) and took in a free music concert—a fun night of conversation, music and dancing under the beautiful night sky at a spectacular golf course near Hua Hin. I was so grateful for these friends and the amazing experiences I've been having with them.

JFDI

January 16th arrived, and I opened my Gmail. I gasped for air. The first edits of my book, *A Year of Love*, came back. I was so overwhelmingly excited and scared shitless about what they were going to say about my work. This is really the first critique of my writing. I had not sent my manuscript to a friend or another author, so I had no idea how it was received.

The editor raved about my topic (love, relationship, self-growth). Ahhh! Something positive. As I curiously read through the remarks, corrections, phrasing changes, grammatical questions, word choices, title questions and so forth, I thought, *I can handle this*. It was another hurdle I accomplished. Another stretch of growing. I was really doing this!

Smooth as a baby's bottom

Scott and I love our coffee, and I found that coffee shops were great for chatting with new people. I met two amazing baristas at the Double U café, and I loved how they loved taking selfies with me. I was meeting new people and learning more about them, which was enriching my life (and theirs as well). It's amazing how you can impact yourself and others when you reach out and talk—and sometimes you never really understand that impact until a later day. It's a beautiful thing.

Getting to meet more people has really been eye-opening. I met the beautiful Poon at a local hair shop down the street from our house. She knew English quite well, and I learned about her and her two adult kids. She's been cutting hair at that shop for about ten years and did a great cut on my hair.

Previous to my haircut with Poon, Scott went there to get a cut and a shave. He came home with a face so smooth, you'd think he never had any whiskers. She charged a great price too! Thank you, Poon, for enriching my life and Scott's too.

Decisions, decisions

I found myself in a new position, something I had never been in before. The school I was now volunteering at offered me a teaching position starting May. Wow, what an opportunity! What an amazing opportunity! However, you know that gut feeling? I was taking the time to listen to it. At first, I thought, *Look at this. It will solve many problems. It will let us stay in Thailand and pay the bills.*

However, the gut feeling leaned towards what it was taking away from me. I felt like I was going back to the grind—five days a week of

January 2023

nine-to-five, all-consuming focus. No time to explore Thailand. Less time with my amazing man. And more exhaustion from teaching all day and not having the energy to put into those important people in my life, including me and my interest in writing books.

I was torn, so I started writing down my pros and cons and thinking it through. I reached out to my PLD course buddy, Shirley. She was studying to be a PD facilitator, and when we connected, she helped me through the thinking process of what I wanted.

In the end, I acknowledged the offer of the teaching position; however, I turned it down.

Later, when I returned to volunteer again, I had a brief encounter with the owner, Padma, and she acknowledged how the staff liked what they saw in me as a volunteer and teacher (even only after a few times at the school). She said I should consider sending in a proposal for the hours I wanted to have a teaching position at HALIO.

I did not believe what I was hearing. My skills and I were desired, and someone was excited to have me write up what I wanted and let them know. This was the part that was so damn mind-blowing for me.

I was now on a mission—to create a proposal for what I really wanted. The choice was actually in my court, which was so foreign to me. I took it on with such vigour that I put the cart before the horse. I sent my first proposal, and then I had a chat with Scott and talked it through a little more. This is something I needed to remind myself. I don't have to jump on things right away. I need to slow down and ask for support and help to think things through.

I went back to my computer and took some time to really think about what I wanted. I knew I wanted to give to kids somehow;

however, I didn't want to go back to the grind of working all day, five days a week.

My final proposal was three full days a week, with the initiative to focus on personal growth and teaching the expected curriculum. I would begin early October (not May, as hoped), when I return to Thailand, as we had already planned a trip back to Canada with return flights to Thailand on September 22, 2023.

Going back home is an extremely important part of my journey and life. I will have a new book, *A Year of Love*, in my hands, and I want to do at least five book launches while in Canada. I also have a huge celebration for this year-long coaching course in early September in the States, and I am not missing that. It comes down to the fact that I have priorities I want to fulfill. I sent in my new proposal and waited for the response. You may be reading this and saying, "You made a mistake, Lisa."

However, what happens is meant to happen.

Working with Scott

At the end of the month, Noi, our landlord, visited us out of the blue. She made a delicious soup for us with some pancakes on the side. Wow! The beautiful gifts we receive when we are open to the beautiful people around us are amazing. Thank you, Noi.

* * *

Scott liked to work at the dining room table of our rental home, so he wouldn't feel stuck in one of the bedrooms. I was aware that I frequented this area a lot, as it was the kitchen. So, I decided to do something for him.

January 2023

One morning, when Scott was volunteering at the elephant sanctuary, I started working on his office, aka our kitchen table. I made a sign that said, "Scott's Office – Online Entrepreneur Forward Walking Choices Coaching." I arranged all his things like one might on their real office desk; however, our eggs and daily supplements were still on it.

When he got the sign I made, he appreciated the gesture—although he tends not to get too excited about these things. I took a picture of him—topless, of course—in his new office, working hard. I love that man.

Now, I was at the point in the coaching course where I was coming to an understanding that I felt Scott and I had this amazing opportunity to work together. I worried, though—and I know worrying does no one any good.

I sat down and brainstormed questions that Scott and I might answer if we recorded a video together. I wanted to see how we would work together in a business situation. I wrote them on paper, cut them apart and thought we could just answer randomly. For several weeks, I had this on my list of goals to accomplish.

We never did this, and it wasn't meant to happen yet. So, all I could do was let him know that I wanted to do this because I felt it's important for both of us to be able to move forward. To see if we *can* work together. To test out if we have the "it" factor to bring to this world.

It's interesting; I feel we have so much to offer this world, yet my own uncertainty about how to make this really happen often comes up. I know that having the answer to what it would look like is unclear—and that should be okay. However, I am still learning to be okay with always taking a risk and JFDI-ing in every situation.

I know Scott appreciates all my skills, all my abilities and all my thoughts, and respects me for me. I know that. Any hesitation I feel in life is always about me, not him. I still have moments, feeling like I'm not good enough, not smart enough, not eloquent enough— and those little nagging stories often have enough clout to make my traction with moving forward in business with Scott.

Do I know I will and I am moving past this? Yes.

Do I know I have it in me? Yes.

Do I know when it will happen? No.

Be gentle to myself. It will happen.

I look back at some pictures of Scott and I together. I see the love we have as I look at Scott's smile. I take the time to look back at mine too. You know what I discovered? It's so genuine. It's so real. It is my superpower. One of my superpowers is my smile.

I look at a pic of Scott swinging on a large root hanging down over the path we were walking on. It brings me such joy when he has moments of being carefree. Like a kid. Just free. And it's so beautiful. It's days like this that I am reminded how grateful I am to be in his presence. My life is beautiful, and I am in the presence of a human being who commits to living his best life every day, even with all the struggles. He brings pure joy to my life. You see it in my smile. And I know his joy is a reflection of my inner beauty too.

We were getting a massage one day, and the masseuse said as she was massaging Scott beside me, "He is happy." She then looked at me and said, "You are happy."

January 2023

It is beautiful that we genuinely love each other, and our energies show it. She further said that we both have a beautiful aura.

It is interesting that when you look around, you see what you want to see. I see love. It was neat to sit in my office (spare bedroom in our rental) and give gratitude for my beautiful life. I soon saw all the hearts in the room that I had not really noticed before. A large one was on the comforter on the bed, and a small one on the spare mattress against the wall. There was also a small, grey heart ornament hanging on the wall. I sure do appreciate my positive thoughts and that I am more in control of what I choose to focus on.

Showing up

Today was a big day! The day for what, you ask? Taking out the scooter all on my own. Ahhhhh! I was really nervous about this; however, today was the day. I made a goal with my coaching course to get out on the scooter. Walk through the fear and just do it.

We have already been in Thailand for four months. That means 120 days of riding on the other side of the road and experiencing a lot of riding on the back of the scooter with Scott. You see, Scott and I have been on longer and shorter rides around town. As for me and my biking experience, I reminded myself of two riding pointers that I learned from my motorcycle classes less than a year ago—look where you are going (not just right in front of you), and turn off the signal light after you put it on.

I can do this. Just breathe.

I decided I needed to ride just around the community area where our house rental was. It was perfect. My biggest learning curve was turning; just coming to a complete stop and turning. So, I went to this back area with no traffic and just practiced and practiced. Signal light on. Brake. Look far where I am turning, keep the eyes on the prize (far where I am turning), and then turn off the signal light. Yes, I got it!

I even felt so great about my progress that I rewarded myself with a coffee at the Debo café, a café I spotted when I was out looking for HALIO school.

I met some great people at Debo. I met Pineapple, a young boy, and his mom who owned the coffee shop. I enjoyed a delicious latte (no sweet!).

Saranya's coffee shop was very delightful. We started chatting; I told her I was volunteering at HALIO, and she shared that Pineapple knew some kids at the school. I asked her if she would appreciate if I came to the coffee shop every Monday after volunteering at HALIO to read with Pineapple. She kindly accepted my offer, and that was the beginning of reading with Pineapple every Monday. It's so amazing how great opportunities arise when I rise.

My first scooter ride to Debo Café in Hua Hin, Thailand

January 2023

What a day—and it was just the beginning of my scootering around Thailand!

I was starting to have a flow come into my life—an understanding that when I do the work, life begins to open up more and more. I've adopted a new reminder that I need to think about those who benefit when I show up. When I remind myself of this, I think of me benefitting, my kids benefitting, my husband benefitting, my family benefitting, my friends benefitting and the world benefitting.

When I show up, the effects are priceless; absolutely mind-blowing, that is for sure.

You may remember the big gala event that happened at the end of our ninety-day goal setting course from my first book. I was determined to show up as the confident woman I knew I was. Now here we were again—in a big year-long course, where we'll be having a big celebration, and I *will* be showing up with amazing things to share about myself and what I've accomplished.

I DMed the course admin and asked if they knew what the theme would be for the gala event. They were unsure, so I decided on the theme—Gold.

Yes, I decided for Scott and me, and he was good with that. We decided to get our outfits tailor-made at a local tailor shop, which was less expensive than back home. So, off we went. After several looks at various tailors, we landed on one with the material we both liked, and they were very helpful and welcoming. It was another one of those JFDI moments.

I (we) made a decision for us, even without the confirmation on the theme. I decided and thought that since the PD company is turning fifty and so am I, gold was just right. Right?

I knew I wanted something that showed I was a strong, confident woman. I wanted something that showed my sexiness. I wanted something that showed I was elegant. So, I chose a gold print top that wrapped up around the back of my neck, a sexy open back and a revealing front that tastefully showed off the girls (and with no bra—ahhh!). The bottom of the dress is black satin, which dropped to the floor, with a high slit up the left side. Glamorous and elegant. I loved it. Now, that's a dress I will rock.

For Scott, he got a whole suit made, and we matched perfectly with a few differences. It was the printed gold material that tied us together. We were super pumped!

GRATITUDE THOUGHT: I SAT IN ANOTHER ROOM WORKING ON MY COMPUTER AS I HEARD SCOTT SPEAK INTO AN APP FOR SPELLING WORDS. I KNOW THAT SPELLING WORDS IS A DAILY CHALLENGE. IT OVERFILLED MY HEART TO KNOW THAT I CONTRIBUTED TO HIS SUCCESS (AS I SPOKE UP AND SUGGESTED THE APP). HE IS A SMART AND CAPABLE MAN.

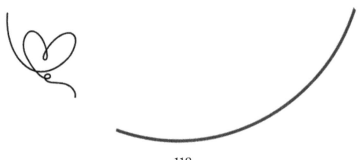

CHAPTER 7

February 2023

I AM INSPIRED, STRONGER, UNCERTAIN, ECSTATIC, CHALLENGED, REFLECTIVE

I signed up for a new challenge—a direct marketing business. I have some good friends who asked me about joining, so the business was credible, and I looked at this as an opportunity to clearly and confidently speak to others.

This business is about enrolment—asking people if they want to be open to learning about this type of business and possibly joining my group and earning extra and residual income. I learned about enrolment in a previous course and about choosing to enroll in personal development work since then. I've been getting braver at asking people and being okay with them saying no.

I was good with the idea of enrolment and enrolling others into the possibility that they would love to be on my team, or at least be a customer. Some days I was psyching myself up for these types of conversations; however, there were more challenges that I did not anticipate when joining this business from the other side of the world.

The time difference was one of those challenges. I was meant to be calling people back in North America, about thirteen hours behind my time in Thailand, because the people I know were there and were the ones I would be asking. Another challenge was the way I could connect. It was recommended to quickly text, "Are you up for a quick call?" and then call when they reply positively. Messenger was my only way to call, and I needed to have those people as friends on Facebook, which made some connections challenging. Yet another challenge was that many who signed up for this, like me, also enrolled themselves into the services which was not something I was able to do, as these types of services are not available in Thailand.

So, I was at a point where I felt like I needed to make a decision about this new business venture I was making. Then, I reassured myself that I needed to be gentle on myself. I knew I would get there. It was going to take time.

Valentine's love

It was almost Valentine's Day, and I thought I would do something nice. I cut out about fifteen hearts and wrote on each of them some special memories Scott and I had. I scattered them all over the bed, along with some flowers from our rental's yard and laid out a sexy, tight-fitting dress I would wear later.

Scott liked the arrangement of these items and thanked me for them. Like I said, I know he doesn't get all excited about such stuff, and this I accept in him. I believe that was part of his upbringing—love and care did not appear much in his life, or at least that's what he felt. I feel a lot of sadness for that young boy robbed of such love.

The kids are coming, the kids are coming!

My kids were finally coming to Thailand! We rented a vehicle for when they arrived. Scott was the brave driver to pick up the car in Hua Hin and drive it in the crazy city of Bangkok. Well, he did a great job. Remember to stay on the left side of the road and adjust to putting the signals on, not the windshield wipers. At least we had clean windows all the time!

When my kids arrived, we stayed fairly close to Hua Hin, taking in the scenery and stopping at local restaurants. Of course, I surprised them at the airport with the shirt I had printed up with our Mother's Day tattoo picture. They thought it was a little embarrassing; I think they were just a little too tired to take it in. Oh, well. It was the thought that counted.

Six Months Of Love

Meeting my kids at the Bangkok airport

We did a lot of activities with the kids, and one that stood out for me was when Scott drove down this back alley that we had accidentally gone down on the scooter before the kids had arrived. Scott knew how much Brianna loved dogs, so we made our way there with the kids, and Brianna got out. Like the dog whisperer she is, they were eating out of her palm in no time. It was so great to see her in her element. I believe Scott felt real good about it too.

Besides the bragging fact that they could say they have visited Thailand, the kids could also tell about the monkey that stole their Pokemon cards. You see, we stopped to show the kids a small temple. Scott and I knew there were a lot of monkeys around there and thought this would be neat for them to experience.

My daughter got out of the car, wearing her mini backpack, and we didn't remind her quickly enough that monkeys will find ways to steal

February 2023

things from her if the opportunity presents itself. And they did. As she got out, the monkey quickly positioned itself on the car, reached inside her opened backpack, and ran off with two sealed packages of Pokemon cards. There was laughter and disbelief, and I believe a little bit of sadness underneath (watching their investment get ripped to shreds).

Another cool story they get to tell was walking with Sweet Honey, an elephant at the Hutsadin Elephant Sanctuary, where Scott volunteered at. Scott specifically started to volunteer at the local elephant sanctuary, so he could give back to the local community and also connect with Brianna, as he knew she was excited to see the elephants. Oh, I almost forgot about the bird shitting on Brianna's new iPhone as she went to see the elephants. Hilarious! Oh, the memories.

Brianna, Jordan, Scott and I with Sweet Honey at the Hutsadin Elephant Foundation in Hua Hin, Thailand

There was also one really special day (for me, at least) with the kids, which had me in tears. Scott and I were walking down the beach, arm in arm, with the two kids walking in front of us, laughing and just being kids—talking, finding shells and tossing coconuts in the water. I absolutely loved it. I watched them laugh and have fun. I was filled with so much love. I was also so grateful that they got to see their mom happy too.

Scott and I also invited the kids to check out our new tailored dress and suit we were finalizing at the tailors. It was neat for them to just experience that; something they may never do in their lives. I know, never say never!

Brianna had a first on this trip. On our hike up the Pa La-U Falls, we bought fish food to feed the fish while walking beside the falls. When we threw in the food, the fish gathered like vultures. With her own bag of food, Brianna got the quorum of fish at her feet on the edge of the water, and after about ten attempts to catch one, she did. Got it on video too!

Oh, the stories to tell, right? Here are a few more! Brianna got to swing on a tree vine, which Jordan and Scott helped her to get up on. She loved the three cows feeding in the field beside our house, discovered a dried-up cockroach and gecko in the door jamb, and played a little bit of pool with Jordan. Oh, and the large monitor lizard that crossed the road in front of the car—Brianna, in her quick-wittedness, quickly got a video. Such cool stories to tell! Let's not forget the amazing caves and the Penis challenge.

Should I tell you or leave you wondering?

Okay, I'll tell you. We were deep in a large cave, and of course, there was an echo. The kids were walking in front of me, and I heard them going back and forth, saying *penis*. I made my way closer to them and asked what they were doing, as the giggles made me wonder.

"It's the Penis challenge," they said.

"What?" I asked, still confused.

They explained that they go back and forth saying penis louder each time, and the person who couldn't go louder after the last one was the loser. Well, I had to see it up close *and* get it on video. I don't remember who won the penis challenge, but we had a great chuckle.

During the kids' trip, I did another Author Retreat with Natasa Denman for this book you're currently reading. This time I was more confident and relaxed and more comfortable speaking in front of the group. I was up each morning at 4 a.m. (for three days) for a seven-hour course. It was perfect timing, as the kids never really woke up until about 11 a.m.

We also went to the beach to see about horseback riding for Brianna; however, the tide was too high that day. We ended up touring a government-run monument of brass statues of Thai kings, which happened to have a well-trained horse that you could take a ride on. Not only a dog whisperer but also a horse whisperer, Brianna rode the majestic horse around, and we got some great pics of her.

Our kids' trip was almost over, so we headed to Bangkok and took in the Sea Life and Wax Museum. Posing with the Obama family and Nicole Kidman was fun, and seeing the sharks and stingrays was amazing. We also hung out at the high-end mall. While the kids made their way around, Scott and I enjoyed some coffee, wherein I saw and took a pic of three couples on the escalator as I sipped my heart-topped latte. Let me explain—my online coach challenged me to notice other couples who displayed love like Scott and me, and to this day, I love this challenge.

It was the night before the kids' flight back to Canada. We had our last meal together, and the next morning, the hotel shuttle took them to the airport. I got in one last picture with them, and I was so overjoyed and grateful for having my kids join me on this adventure and holding my babies again.

An emotional day

After dropping off the kids and travelling back to Hua Hin, one of Scott's buddies, Rob, arrived. He was on an adventure in Thailand for a month and stayed with us for a few days. We visited a 50-year-old teak structure called The Sanctuary of Truth.

At this amazingly beautiful spot, I heard about George (a Canadian friend of Scott's) and how his dog had succumbed to an injury earlier in the week. It's interesting how some things affect you the way they do. You see, I only connected with George via Facebook because of Scott. I followed him and his life and adventures with his dog, Smokey. I never met George (or Smokey, for that matter); however, I found it important to reflect, close my eyes and send my love to George. I sat down in the teak Sanctuary of Truth, opened up my palms and sent George all the love I could. I appreciate that I took the time to reflect and send my condolences to George for the loss of Smokey. After a minute or so, I continued through the amazing structure of intricate carvings.

After venturing to Pattaya with Rob and then saying our goodbyes to him, Scott and I ventured to the Bridge Over the River Kwai. It was a very emotionally draining day walking over the river, knowing that many people died there during World War II. Scott found himself having a lot of emotions and reflected on that.

I did not have such an emotional day; I'm not sure why, and I don't compare myself to Scott. However, a few things came into play that day. I had just been with my kids and was feeling sadness and joy all at the same time. Also, I was feeling a sense of uncertainty over the direction I was taking in my life, feeling in a sense of limbo. Moving around a lot was also taking some toll on me and the sleep and rest I was getting (or lack there of).

I also have been troubled for years with not fully feeling my feelings when they happen. I'm just now discovering how to really let go and feel. I've been suppressing feelings (at least the extremes of joy and sadness) for most of my life, and I'm still discovering more about this. Was it because of my role as a teacher, as a mother? Was it because I never felt support in showing my feelings? Probably it's a combination of all those things. Well, now I'm aware and practicing to let go, to feel. And best of all, Scott is my biggest supporter in this new area of growth.

Back in Hua Hin

It was Tiky's birthday when we arrived back in Hua Hin, and we celebrated on the rooftop of the Sky Bar Hotel. Both the view and Tiky were very stunning. Scott ate beef wellington for the first time and shared the large meal with his buddy, John. He said it was one of the best things he had ever eaten. I would say it better be good when you have the chef himself bring it out to show you before carving it for you.

It's funny how sometimes it's the little things you don't really think about. You see, I was attending one of the many online workshops, and we got on the topic of signing our books and what to write on the inside cover. So, I got out a piece of paper and wrote, "Enjoy reading, Lisa Brearly." I looked at it and realized, *Oops, I forgot an* E.

I wrote it again. "Enjoy reading, Lisa Brearley."

Even though I had been married to Scott for seven months at that point, I never physically wrote my name, Lisa Brearley, with a pen. You may remember I didn't change any paperwork before I left and kept my last name Maze (passport, credit cards, etc.). I sure have some practicing to do.

Forgot to mention a very important experience that I had during this month. While Rob was in Hua Hin, he rented a scooter and decided not to ride it. Since it was already rented, Scooter Mama (yeah, me!) got to get more practice. I was out on the main roads, travelling around 80 km/h, and I was doing great! Wow, stretching that comfort zone again! JFDI!

february 2023

GRATITUDE THOUGHT: AS I WORKED AWAY ON MY COMPUTER IN THE SPARE BEDROOM, SCOTT WAS MAKING HIMSELF A COFFEE AND TALKING TO HIS BROTHER, TED (WHOM HE RECONNECTED WITH AFTER TWENTY-FIVE YEARS). I HEARD SCOTT SAY ABOUT TED'S DAUGHTER, TARA, "I WANT TO LET YOU KNOW, TED, I'M VERY PROUD OF HER."

I LOVE THIS ABOUT SCOTT. HE KNOWS WHAT TO SAY AND WHAT IS MEANINGFUL. I HAVE COME TO UNDERSTAND THAT SPEAKING FROM THE HEART IS EXTREMELY IMPORTANT IN MY LIFE. THANK YOU, SCOTT.

CHAPTER 8

March 2023

I AM GRATEFUL, DOUBTFUL, CERTAIN, EXCITED, BLESSED

Tiky was excited to show us a new restaurant. Each table was on its own dock in the middle of a pond—very cool. The food was good too. We later ventured back to that restaurant for my birthday dinner, where I asked for only Scott and me to go. It was a lovely evening with all the white lights lit up around the pond area and music playing. It was also a little cooler after the sun went down compared to when John, Tiky, Scott and I went during the heat of the day.

I've loved my time here in Thailand. I'm getting out with new friends I have met and tested and tried out new things—new food, driving a scooter on the other side of the road and speaking a new language.

I was invited for a drive out to Cha-am to hang out with some of my new female Thai friends for some home cooking again. We also went to a large night market where they sold some of their clothes and household items. I had fun helping them out and speaking with strangers interested in what we were selling. I'm starting to see what I bring to my friends and how we all benefit when I "show up."

A few days later I got to hang out with Tiky, Nam and a new friend, Noi (yes, same name as our landlord), for a home-cooked meal. They made steamed fish and veggies, papaya salad and sticky rice. I tried out new veggies, like bamboo shoots—hmmm, it was okay. In previous gatherings with the ladies, I chimed in every so often during their Thai conversation, and they translated once in a while to fill me in on their topic of discussion. Most of them knew some English, but not very fluently. This time, I got smart. I kept the Google Translate app open on my phone while they chatted. I caught some bits and pieces of what they talked about, so I could participate better in the conversation. After, the four of us went out for coffee. I got to show Noi how to record a video on TikTok. What a fab day with them!

Grateful

On March 13, it was my last day volunteering at HALIO and reading with Pineapple at the local coffee shop. I was truly blessed to have these opportunities, and it reminded me how rich my life is. How grateful am I to be able to give back and share myself and my skills as a teacher.

The principal at HALIO asked me to meet with him over lunch and assured me we would stay in contact if there was an opening at the school. One thing I knew was that I would love to return to the school to volunteer. I loved how students were seen as leaders of their learning and were happy to be at school.

It was my last day with Pineapple too. His mom, Saranya, was so gracious and kind. I had a small selection of books that I would bring to read both at the school and with Pineapple. I asked him to choose his favourite book. It was *Chicka Chicka Boom Boom*. At the end of our session, I gave him that book and made sure to give his mom the children's book with English and Thai words I bought off Lazada (the Amazon of Thailand).

Saranya gave me her thanks every time I read with her son. I appreciated the opportunity and the iced latte (no sugar) she made for me each time. This final time, she gave me a T-shirt from the surf shop she also owns down on the beach. It's called the Pineapple Surf Club, named after her son. I am truly a blessed woman to have had them as a part of my life journey and adventure here in Thailand.

I'm so happy with myself for stretching my comfort zone and seeing if Pineapple and his mom were interested in me reading with him every week. Saranya once told me that after our first few times reading together, Pineapple would excitedly get up the next day and ask, "Is that lady coming today?"

Expanding my comfort zone brought me to wonderful people like Pineapple's family and the staff and students at HALIO.

Experiencing doubt

I signed up to give back in the area of personal growth. The personal development course that Scott and I first met at and have done a lot of work through often requests the graduates to volunteer and take on the staffing role.

With the way my life was at this point, previously busy as a school teacher and now travelling, I had not had the opportunity to staff a basic three-day personal development weekend. So, while in Thailand I signed up as a volunteer for the beginner three-day personal development seminar, which was almost within a week of us arriving back home in Canada. However, I was doubting if I could truly commit and give my all; doubting that I could participate as fully as possible, mostly for two reasons. For one, I was still halfway across the world, and calling and connecting had been such a struggle. As well, the three-day event was happening in Vancouver, and I knew only one person who lived there, so who could I call to attend the course?

Was it doubt, or was it fear? Was I scared to enroll others? Was I scared to tell this group of staffing volunteers that I was doubtful of my capabilities to contribute in finding attendees for this personal development course? What was it exactly? A sprinkle of all those things, I suppose!

I stated my concern with the whole group about enrolling people into the course from so far away and not knowing anyone in that area who could attend. And, of course, because I was brave and spoke up regarding my concerns, another lady stated the same challenge. It was my reminder to always speak up.

I found that when I am honest and open with myself and share with others, the best results happen. You see, one goal of mine over the past few years in all this personal development work was to be okay with contributing my thoughts and feelings in any situation. This has been a long time coming, and it's finally becoming more comfortable. I continue to be open to solutions to support the group as much as I can. To do what I can. To attend what I can. I also know that I am capable of many things.

March 2023

Fifty

A big milestone was coming up for me—turning fifty. I was both excited and stunned. What? When did that all happen? Where did the time go?

Scott and I went out for my last dinner as a 49-year-old woman. Ironically, the table we sat at had a picture of an old train with the words *Saskatchewan* on it—a province in Canada. We treated ourselves to some roti with banana and Nutella from the lady who makes delicious roti and donairs, whom we have visited about five times now. She is such a hard worker and is so delightful. Every time we visited, she greeted us with a big smile, which was hidden behind the mask but we knew was there. She was always so welcoming and kind. She spoke little English, but her way of being was what we loved the best. It was always worth the wait to get her food and, most importantly, be part of her caring nature. She has surely made an impression on us, and I'm so grateful to have met her on this journey.

My fiftieth birthday arrived. Noi, our landlord, visited with a beautiful bouquet of flowers. Absolutely gorgeous! She is another person I am grateful to have been part of my journey in life and in Thailand. She is a giving and kind soul.

I know and remind myself that I meet these people because of who I am and how I show up. It's the energy I give out. It's the love that even Scott and I exude when we are together. I know others appreciate and love our powerful energy and love for each other, and we attract those types of people because of our authentic love.

* * *

Scott and I agreed not to buy presents for each other, and this birthday was no different. It was all about time and experiences together, so off we went for my birthday lunch. The restaurant we ate at was first introduced to us by John and Tiky. Its tables were in their own little cabanas, surrounded by the lush greenery of trees and brick paths. One thing I appreciate is the time we spend outside eating. This is one thing we have little of in Canada. In Thailand, restaurants can operate outside all year round, so eating outside is normal.

While we ate stir-fry and curry soup, I got a text from Saranya, asking if I was home. She mentioned she wanted to drop something off at our house rental for my birthday. I told her we were out for lunch and agreed to come see her at the Pineapple Surf Club. Who would pass up going to a restaurant on the beach?

Saranya was worried that she was putting us out of our way, so I assured her we love going to new places and exploring. And we really did! That is another thing I love about Scott and me—exploring, looking at new things, going to new places and being amazed by what we discover.

After punching into the GPS, we took the twenty-minute ride to the Surf Club. Upon stepping foot onto the beach, we saw surfers out in the water and Pineapple (yes, the 6-year-old) out on his own surfboard. I waved to him, and we made our way up to the restaurant. Scott helped Pineapple carry his board, as it looked like he was struggling. However, we later saw him carry it with ease. It was great seeing Scott step up that way, and I believe Pineapple appreciated the gesture.

Saranya treated us to delicious iced coffees and homemade chips and salsa. The people of Thailand have been so kind. We chatted with some customers and relaxed in the lounge chairs. It was a beautiful experience. After an hour or so, I mentioned to Saranya that we needed the bill and would be on our way. She had mentioned an ice cream cake and quickly got that organized. She lit candles, and everyone sang. Because of the heat, the ice cream cake was quickly melting. We were all glad to share the cake on that hot day.

Saranya did not charge us for anything we had eaten, though Scott insisted on giving the server a tip. It was truly very special, and even as I write, the emotions of gratitude are swelling in my eyes. I felt a lot of love on this day. It's something I will never forget.

I forgot to tell you how my morning started on such a high note! My daughter was the first family member to wish me a happy birthday. As I mentioned, she and I were connected on Snapchat, and I saw her birthday wishes first. She's another person I am so grateful for in my life. I am so overfilled with joy that my relationship with my daughter seems to grow and expand. It is truly a blessing.

My birthday fun was not yet done. Scott and I headed to the mall, as I wanted to get a new dress for my big birthday dinner the next evening with our Thai group of friends. When we arrived at the mall, I thought I would appreciate some time looking and wandering around at my pace, as I enjoyed shopping. Meanwhile, Scott suggested he'd go for a massage. What two great ideas!

I enjoyed my time alone, shopping and wandering, knowing I would find a dress. My first stop was a store with various dresses arranged as if it was a second-hand store—no multiple dresses, only an understanding that this rack was a certain size. I was greeted by a young saleswoman whom I had a conversation with (the best we could with the language challenges) and learned she was 19 years old and taking higher education. She was a great help, and I loved how kind and attentive she was, holding the four dresses I decided to try on.

My heart was on the warm peach silky dress with flowers and a plunging neckline. After I tried it on, I asked the young lady to keep it aside while I looked around the mall a little more, and then I would return to tell her if I would get it. She kindly obliged.

After wandering around without seeing anything else out there and, of course, stopping to get a coffee, I returned to the store. I tried on the dress one more time and bought it. The saleswoman even gave me a discount. Wow! Life is amazing. I think the dress cost me under CAN$30.

My amazing man was all massaged up, and I had my dress. What a great few hours! My overwhelming feeling of gratitude was not over yet. I got a text from Saranya, saying there was a surprise at our house rental.

After our dinner out at that restaurant on the pond, we headed home and, to my surprise, something yellow was attached to the sliding gate. Pineapple and his mom dropped off a yellow smiley face balloon and attached it to the gate. How did I know Pineapple was there to drop it off? Saranya later sent a picture of Pineapple holding the balloon before they attached it to the gate. Wow! I think about that amazing gesture. I am truly blessed in my life.

March 2023

Thank you, Pineapple, for the smiley-faced balloon for my 50th birthday.

All day I was reminded that showing how much you care for others is extremely important. Going the extra mile for the important people in your life is a must. I love that Pineapple's family has reminded me of this. Thank you.

It's interesting how you build relationships with others when you share. Scott and I have shared a lot about the coffee shops we've frequented over our time here in Thailand. We posted about some very interesting ones, and when we share, others connect. Our Calgary friend, Carrie-Anne, texted one day, "You and Scott should open your own coffee shop." Well, I joked we should, as we both love our coffee. In the back of my mind, I knew I would find the right coffee shop sign that Scott and I could take our picture in front of, as if it was our own place.

Shortly after Carrie-Anne's comment, I saw the coffee shop. We never stopped that day, but we drove by it probably about ten times after that. Each time we passed by I always looked at it and knew I would stop there and take a selfie in front of the sign (Okay, I can hear Scott saying, "It's not a selfie if it's the two of us." Oh, babe).

Well, we were riding down by that coffee shop again, and I asked Scott to pull over, and we took our selfie. I sent the photo to Carrie Ann. She commented that she loved the name of "our" restaurant, Coffee Love. It was a perfect name for us and our new coffee restaurant. Right?

Our Coffee Love restaurant

March 2023

Connection awareness

About a month ago I met a lovely lady who opened a new massage shop close to one Scott was at as I was waiting for him at a nearby coffee shop. I started talking to her as she was taking a break. She told me her name was Rabbit and offered a free massage on my birthday, so it was time to take her up on it. Unfortunately, we missed her on my actual birthday. However, the next day Scott and I got the absolute best massage ever. I am so grateful and proud of myself for stepping up and talking to her that day. I now recognize this in myself and acknowledge that I am doing things differently and getting different results.

As I said, the massage was amazing, and she is more knowledgeable and educated about the body than we have experienced with other Thai massages. It was great to have someone knowledgeable and able to identify that Scott has a "sugar problem" when she was massaging his legs. And yes, we did not speak about his diabetes to her at all. She focussed on areas that needed more attention, like my left shoulder blade area. She gave tips on what to do at home to promote flexibility and stretch muscles that really needed extra attention.

My massage with Rabbit was almost spiritual. She massaged my stomach and commented, "You had babies, right?"

I nodded. It was like she was really taking care of me—nurturing the person I was, what I've lived through and who I was rediscovering. Tears began to fall down my ears. It was a beautiful experience. Thank you, Rabbit, for that absolutely wonderful and grounding experience.

We recommended Rabbit to John and Tiky. They later went and thought she did a great job too. I love that I am more aware of the amazing people that have come into my life. This awareness started a few years back with a young girl named Diamond.

Diamond received a cancer diagnosis when she was a student in my kindergarten class. She passed away about four years later, and I soon realized after her death, in all the pain of seeing her leave this earth, that I was truly grateful to have known her. I now speak highly of her and how she positively affected my life. I like to remember her now as my diamond in the sky. It puts a smile on my face to continue to "Shine Bright Like Diamond." That just might be my next written tattoo!

I have come to better appreciate when amazing people come into my life. I will talk about them. I light up when I do. Many might say they saw this in me when I spoke about Scott. He, like Diamond, is a truly amazing soul that I am so grateful to have met.

The massage and my birthday dinner were all on the day after my actual birthday. We went home after the massage and got ready for dinner at the same restaurant (Nai Lert Beach House) where we celebrated Scott's birthday back in October. (Remember Scott's birthday is the same date as my son's birthday?)

Our amazing Thai friends met us there, and we enjoyed dinner on the beach. They gave me thoughtful gifts: a beautiful silver bracelet (love my silver jewellery), a book on Thai phrases and a pen for writing my signature on all my books. I am so blessed by how thoughtful others are. What a perfect evening! Thank you, friends.

March 2023

*My 50th birthday celebration dinner with our new friends—
Tiky (Thitaphorn), John, Nam (Sukanya) and Terry*

It is important to connect with others and meet new people and find out about them. My advice: Get to know more people.

Another great birthday memory was when I video called my daughter on Snapchat. She was just stopping by to see her brother, so I got to talk to both kids and see Jordan's new wheels. He had bought a new car since arriving in Thailand, and it was not in use since it was winter in Canada and not winter-ready. On this day, he got it out. Wow, I love seeing my kids and how they are growing up. I'm a very proud Mama!

Stepping into fears and risks

I was on my journey with the year-long coaching course; almost ninety days in at this point. I haven't spoken of it much; however, it consists of stretching my comfort zone and working towards my big goal. My revised goal over this time frame was to create an experience of confidence building, risk-taking and sharing my emotions. I was to share *A Year of Love* with at least five live audiences and five book launches. My goal was to be completed before the big celebration in September, and I was bound and determined to do it.

I've really been stepping into fears and risks—doing live videos, asking others to purchase my book, feeling confident to call myself an author. It's been a big swing forward for me. Don't get me wrong, I have days of self-doubt and "I can't do this"; however, I know those are my past stories and beliefs. I look at them and find the courage to see and put them to the side, so I can continue striving to move forward in my life.

Last days in Hua Hin

We spent our last two days in Hua Hin with our friends, visiting coffee shops and scootering around. Our wonderful landlord, Noi, invited us for dinner, so we met her at a local restaurant. It has been a pleasure renting from her. She is a wonderful lady, and we are grateful to have met her.

March 2023

GRATITUDE THOUGHT: SCOTT AND I WERE AT THE BIKE GARAGE, GETTING OUR SCOOTER TIRE FIXED. HE WAS CHECKING OUT WHAT THE MECHANIC WAS DOING, THEN CAME OVER TO KISS ME AS I SAT ON THE BENCH NEARBY. I APPRECIATE THE COMBINATION OF HIS SENSITIVE AND RUGGED SIDE.

CHAPTER 9

April 2023

*I AM OPEN, REFLECTIVE, GRATEFUL, GIVING.
(HOME IS WHEREVER I CHOOSE.)*

We rode up to Bangkok the next day with Tiky and John in their truck to hang out during our last few days in Thailand. It has been wonderful getting to know and hanging out with them. Our experiences with them were fun and filled with many coffee stops! We hope to see you again soon, guys!

We left a few bags at the Bangkok Hotel and headed off to Cambodia by plane, knowing it was the last part of this leg in South Asia. We spent several days exploring Angkor Wat in Siem Reap, then headed off to Phnom Penh. It was in Cambodia's capital where we visited the killing fields. This Genocide Museum—such an emotional few days—was one of the most moving and impressionable experiences for both of us during this six-month travel.

Back in Thailand, we went on our last big adventure—Koh Chang, Thailand. We met with a Canadian buddy, Cliff, and his Thai wife, Siri. We took a ferry to the island, and after a 30-minute cab ride, we arrived at the Cliff Cottage Resort (funny enough, no connection to our buddy, Cliff). This was an absolutely incredible spot. Just google it, and you will see that out the front of the room was where the sun rose over the beach; out the back, where the restaurant was, was where the sun set over the rocky shore.

Life has surely been an amazing journey—one that I am so grateful for. I now am more aware of the beauty around me and more appreciative of the amazing people I have met.

The people we met at the Cliff Resort took care of us over the next eight days. We had fun joking with the bartender about singing to us as we caught her singing some Thai songs out loud several times. We had a fabulous time exploring Koh Chang with Clifford and Siri. We got to experience a Thai Boxing event, which was a blast! And thanks to Cliff and Siri, we explored amazing back roads on the scooter and just lived the best life there for eight days.

I almost forgot to talk about a very memorable experience I had with Scott here in Koh Chang. He had decided on a tattoo, which honoured those people he knew who had passed away and had an effect on his life. It was a huge tattoo that covered his whole side. The tattoo was a tree, which represented a friend who had passed and the names of others who also passed away on the roots—an amazing way to acknowledge those beautiful souls. He went through a lot of pain in the upper part of that tattoo.

Later when we arrived back in Canada, Scott had a moment where he was describing the tattoo to someone asking about it, and he broke down. He realized the only way to be added to his tattoo was to have

April 2023

an important connection to him and, of course, would have died. That deep understanding hit home for him. That was an emotional moment for him, but a beautiful one at the same time.

Back at the Cliff Resort, we made our daily videos with mountainous jungle hills in the background. My videos were for me to be seen, heard and noticed and for others to get to know me a little more (especially if my book is going to go anywhere). The bottom line was that doing these videos also got me to step up and expand my comfort zone. For Scott, he is getting his online coaching business out there. He made daily videos about his wisdom and what he offers as a coach—not in any pushy way, but in a way that shows how his past experiences offer support for others.

* * *

Scott and I took in a beautiful sunset one night. All my life I appreciated the little things, and I'm learning to understand that they are not the little things but rather the important things. The things that are at my core. The things that, without, life would not be rich.

Cliff Resort was really cool. We had the beach (although not suitable for swimming) out our front door, and out back was the rocky beach that was great for snorkelling. We had our daily breakfast on the cliffside, and I often was inspired by Scott. He would go off to the rocky beach and sit on a rock and just be with himself, so he could record the daily videos he posted on his YouTube channel, Forward Walking Choices Coaching.

Each video he recorded had a message. He shared his video with me after he recorded it. I make this notice because I am still in a place of seeing what I have to say as important enough to share and that I can get my thoughts and feelings across in a cohesive manner. This I continue to work on. I am grateful that Scott asks me to watch his videos.

After recording his videos, Scott often says, "I'm not sure if that was very good." However, I found his videos were often very powerful. Each showed a man being brave and vulnerable. Each showed a man who knew what he had to share was important. His inspiring videos helped encourage me to continue with my videos and keep expressing myself.

I see my husband as a very influential and inspirational man. I've spoken with others who have felt this too. His heart is one of the biggest I've encountered in my life. His dedication to move forward is sitting right on that big heart. He, like me, is on a journey, and I respect the journey he is on and what he needs to do.

I'm still learning how to show up for my husband. How to show and share my authentic self. I am still discovering myself, and I'm open to pushing myself to reveal that. I say "reveal that" because I know it has been inside me all this time; it just got lost along the way.

I am proud to say I am still discovering my authentic self. I am worth the journey to discover the complete person inside me. Reaching some pinnacle of completeness does not really exist because I continue to be in a state of learning, no matter what age.

Stretching my comfort zone is both exciting and scary. It's scary because I question if I can maintain this level of growth. I question whether I can keep pushing myself. I have come to understand that there is no unlearning. My experiences have brought me to a new level, a new awareness. To compare this thought, I think of the Healthy Transformations Program I'm part of with Dr. Michael Breen and Mr. Christopher Lawrence. All the facts and knowledge I have learned about food, support my decision to eat healthy because, in the end, my body and mind will thank me. I cannot unlearn the knowledge I've learned about food and the understanding I've experienced about myself.

April 2023

Oh, the things I have learned

I want to share a really amazing experience while in Thailand. As you have read, I met some great Thai ladies who introduced me to Thai lottery. I've never really played the lottery and was excited about winning. At the same time, I was happy these two ladies, Tiky and Siri, spoke up and suggested it.

Because they spoke up, it created a fantastic chain reaction. I first thought, *Who else can benefit from this lottery if I won?* and immediately thought of my kids. Actually, to tell the truth, I immediately offered those two ladies part of the winnings, too, and then Snapchatted the kids.

I told Jordan and Brianna about the big lotteries—the first being CAN$400,000, and the second CAN$1.1 million. I told them I would share it with them if they emailed me three things: I wanted to know what (and how much) they would spend it on, what they would invest it in and where they would tithe their money. I needed to know what they would do with the money, which I wanted in writing.

This was such a great exercise; I found out what was important to them and created new ways to communicate and understand them. Unfortunately, I (we) did not win. However, I won on a much deeper level. What a blessing!

This is a reminder to myself (and now to you because you are reading my book) that when I connect with others (and I'm sure many of you are like me and are scared to speak up), I never know who I'm going to positively affect.

Our last leg

We were on the last leg of our journey in Thailand, and I could sense from Scott that going back to Canada felt somewhat unpleasant or unwanted for him. I made sure to talk with him about it and was open to the space he needed to process this for himself. Meanwhile, I was looking forward to seeing my kids, my parents, my siblings and my friends in person. I was also scared because I was in the next stage of more book promotion—the book launches! So, it was both exciting and scary for me all at the same time. I am so grateful for the amazing memories. I am learning how to show up differently in my life, how others truly benefit when I do show up.

The last stop of our Thailand adventure was Bangkok, and we chose a hotel that was quiet and gave us space to just decompress before heading back home.

If you are a Canadian, you may know that April is that time of year—tax time. I've never done my own taxes before. My former husband did a great job at that, and I was never part of filing taxes, except to give my T4 slip to him and remind him of my SIN number. Here's a new experience that I was about to learn. Well, kind of.

You see, Scott worked with Julie, our friend who loved karaoke and played the music at our wedding (Remember Julie? You met her in my first book *A Year of Love*). She was supporting me in doing my taxes. Thank goodness I was more confident asking for support when I needed it. This is also something I've learned over the last few years: It's okay to ask for support. It's okay to not know everything. It's okay to be in a position of learning. And it's okay to find this challenging. JFDI and ask for help.

April 2023

Back on Canadian soil

Scott and I boarded the plane just after midnight on April 7. After the almost 30-hour journey back to Vancouver, Canada, we were greeted by our great friend, Mark and 15 lb Jack Russell, Norton. Wow, Norton's tail was wagging like crazy! It was great to see Mark in person, too, and not just over video.

We were back in Canada, and now what? I knew I was changing what I wanted to do in life in terms of my career. I had realized over the last few months that going back to the classroom was something I was not interested in doing. So, now what? I know I liked seeing other places in the world and really experiencing them. I know I also loved the creativity of writing books. I also know I was pushing myself in new areas of my life.

As I mentioned, I was now an independent business owner (IBO) with a direct marketing company that partnered with companies for comparable services and prices. I joined this 30-year-old company at the end of January and did my best to step into that arena. You see, I always thought of this marketing technique as a very scary arena. A place where I had to be heard, seen and trusted. I take this new challenge on and stretch this comfort zone of mine.

To create a win-win for me and push myself to step up to the plate as an IBO, I decided to walk downtown of our small town and see if local business owners would like to see what I offer. I walked in and introduced myself and what I had to offer. Several owners were open to the conversation, and it was good practice for me.

It has been a big learning experience to speak up. I know that this stretching is great for me. I know it's been a fear, and now I'm finding it a bit more comfortable.

The weekend with a breakthrough

About a week after we returned home, I had a big breakthrough in realizing how I was showing up for others. I volunteered as a staff member for that personal development class and spent three long but powerful days entrenched in PD work. This weekend was twofold. The first was to lead a small group in their personal growth journey and write up all the posters plastered around the room for information and reminders. The second part was to personally benefit from retaking this class and be open to more discovery of that authentic, complete person in me.

One of my students in the small group was Frederic. He, along with five other members, created goals, and when I asked him, he mentioned his relationship with his wife.

"What does she like?" I asked him.

"She loves surprises," he said.

"What does she like?" I asked again.

"Chocolate," he quickly replied. "I'm thinking of getting her chocolates."

I kind of stopped him there. "Frederic," I said, "can I suggest you don't think about it and just do it after our class tonight?"

Well, Frederic did just that.

I told Frederic that he had inspired me. Because he shared this with me, he inspired me to really *be with* my husband that evening, after a long and emotionally charged day. You see, I was really tired, having

April 2023

just returned to Canada with a 13-hour time difference, and it was only day six of that, plus the long hours I was putting in to volunteer for these amazing people who attended this personal development class.

So, I had a choice. Frederic inspired me to JFDI. I knew I was tired, yet I decided to show up for my husband when he picked me up after the class, and we went to a restaurant to meet his friends, many of whom I was meeting for the first time.

After asking Frederic to JFDI, he told me that his wife was surprised and happy with his efforts. I'm happy for Frederic. Thank you, Frederic, for positively impacting me too.

After this conversation with Frederic, I was more inspired to connect and be really *present* with the attendees in the course. I spent that weekend experiencing such joy—and yes, there were many tears. It was a beautiful weekend.

I am grateful to be back in Canada because there are so many amazing opportunities for me. I had a beautiful conversation with my kids, my sister and Scott when we had dinner together. I say it's a beautiful conversation because I have an open mind and heart to those who want the best for me. It was a conversation around stepping up to share my knowledge and concern about my children understanding how to make and manage money to become financially independent and confident. I could have chosen to take that conversation with the perspective that I am a poor mom, a poor money manager and that I failed my kids. Don't get me wrong, I had that initial thought; however, I realized I can stand up for my kids now. Do I have all the answers? No. Do I love my kids? Yes, and that's why I will step forward with these important conversations. I planned a future conversation with my kids regarding money. I want them to take on responsibility for their bills, learn how to budget their money and understand where it goes.

It scares me to have a conversation around money because my former husband did all the money management, and I am slowly learning how to manage my own money. I know this conversation will be about sharing the fact that this learning curve is also happening to me. Most importantly, I'm stepping through this fear of talking to my kids about this because I choose to step up so they can benefit (and I know I will too).

Time to close this chapter

I could go on and on about my amazing life and the understandings that I have gained. However, my book is coming to an end.

This book will not end with a wedding or some big event, like in my first book. It will end with these extremely important messages:

Each one of us is worth everything that is possible. Each one of us is complete on the inside. Each one of us has come to believe the stories we were told, reconfirmed them during our lifetime, and understanding we are capable of starting anew. Each one of us needs to live like it is our last day on earth or our first.

With these thoughts, I ask you: Who will benefit when you show up?

Each one of us can ask for support and give support. Are you feeling lost? Connect with someone else.

You are worth it.

You deserve it.

Yes, you.

April 2023

Yes, I am worthy.

GRATITUDE THOUGHT: THANK YOU, COACH MATT, FOR THIS EXTREMELY IMPORTANT REMINDER: *OPTIMUM RESULTS ARE ONLY AVAILABLE WHEN YOU HAVE ZERO EXPECTATIONS ON THE OUTCOME.*

Calls to Action

1. Email Lisa at lgallant1973@gmail.com and Lisa will send you a FREE Confidence Builder Blueprint.

2. Book Lisa Brearley (https://forwardwalkingchoices.com) for an online presentation of her inspiring personal growth journey and how she shows up for herself and her husband. Key takeaways: Taking control, choosing to expand your comfort zone, and gratitude. Click on "Let's Chat"

3. Book Lisa and Scott Brearley (https://forwardwalkingchoices.com) for an online presentation on their own personal stories and journey of growth, and discover how they show up for each other in their relationships. Click on "Let's Chat" and let's get connected.

Acknowledgements

With gratitude being one of the heightened awarenesses in my life comes the level of acknowledgement of the many who have graced my life. First of all, my soulmate, Scott. Thank you for being the man who shows me daily what love is and respects me as I go through my personal journey of growth.

I am blessed with two beautiful children, Jordan and Brianna, and an amazing family I was born into. The love I experienced in my life reminds me to find ways to love them even more each day.

A big thank you to the kind and gracious Carrie-Anne for taking care of my 80 lb dog, Alya, while I was away in Thailand. She and her kids loved Alya like their own. Forever thankful to Carrie-Anne, Wallace and Sawyer.

My gratitude and acknowledgement is extended to Natasa Denman, founder of the Ultimate 48 Hour Author, whose experience and mastered skills in the authoring process have contributed to making my own authoring journey a success. Working with the U48HA crew and being a part of this author community has been a blessing.

I'm blessed with all the people I've connected with in my life. Every encounter is a blessing and a chance to challenge myself to show up. I acknowledge my own perseverance and the dedication that I put into my book and my life.

About the Author

Lisa Brearley is a beautiful woman, partner, mother and public system teacher for almost twenty years. Now she's a world traveller and published author. In 2023, Lisa published her first book, *A Year of Love*.

As a second-time author, Lisa is excited about her life and sharing her experiences and growth. Her inspiring journey in finding her voice and experiencing and celebrating challenges, failures and successes pushes Lisa forward to live her best life ever. For Lisa, life is about constantly updating, expanding and deciding what to keep and what to let go of.

When not in Thailand, Lisa resides in the quaint little village of Ashcroft, British Columbia, Canada with her husband, Scott.

Join Lisa in *Six Months of Love* as she explores Thailand with her husband, Scott. Through her honest, open and revealing experiences, Lisa's journey will make connections with every reader.

Six Months of Love, sequel to *A Year of Love*, is packed with life-changing experiences filled with gratitude and Lisa's improved clarity on what makes life worth living.